RESOLUTIONS

PASSED BY THE

TRUSTEES OF COLUMBIA COLLEGE;

WITH

BRIEF NOTICES OF THE ACTION OF THE
BOARD UPON IMPORTANT SUBJECTS,

FROM

1820 TO 1868.

NEW YORK:
D. VAN NOSTRAND, No. 192 BROADWAY.

1868.

CONTENTS.

	PAGE
Board of trustees	3
Standing committee	4
Committee on course of instruction	4
Committee on the school of mines	4
Committee on the school of law	5
Committee on the library	5
Committee on honors	5
Resolution directing the preparation of this synopsis	7
Academical dress	9, 155
Appropriations, special	10
Appropriations, permanent	12
Attendance at prayers	14, 155
Botanical garden	14
Erection of college buildings	16
College building, site for	17
College buildings, use of	17
Catalogue	17
Chemistry, department of	19
Church site, lots reserved for	22
Cloak room	23
Commencements and exhibitions	23
Diplomas	25
Elocution, instruction in	26, 153
Examinations	28, 157
Fees	29
Financial policy, permanent	31

CONTENTS.

	PAGE
Free tuition	36, 158
Gebhard fund	36
Grammar school	37
Greenwood cemetery	41
Herbarium	42
Honors	44
Inquiry into the state of the college, committee on	44
Instruction, course of, and committee on the course	48
Inventory of movable property	66
Law school	66
Library	75
Medicine, school of	84
Merit rolls	87
Meteorological observations	87
Military education	88
Mines, school of	89
Minutes of the board	109
Modern languages	110
Natural history, lyceum of	111
Observatory, astronomical	111
President, of the	112
Prize scholarships and prizes	113, 158
Professorships and professors	117
Reading-room	125
Repairs	126, 162
Reviews of studies	126
Salaries	127
Seal	133, 162
Scholarships, free	134
Smithsonian institution, agreement with	136
Societies, college	137
Sports and games	138
Standing committee	138
Transfer of students from class to class	144

CONTENTS.

	PAGE
Treasurer, of the	144, 166
Trustees	145, 166
Tutorships	151
University convocation	153
Visitation of the college	153
Weights, measures, and coins	154

SUPPLEMENTARY.

Chair of governor Clinton	156
Prize fellowships and scholarships	158
Removal of the college	162

COLUMBIA COLLEGE.

BOARD OF TRUSTEES.

NAMES.	RESIDENCES.
HAMILTON FISH, LL. D., Chairman of the Board	251 East 17th Street.
GARDINER SPRING, S. T. D., LL. D	6 West 37th "
SAMUEL B. RUGGLES, LL. D	24 Union Square.
WILLIAM BETTS, LL. D., Clerk	122 East 30th Street.
BENJAMIN I. HAIGHT, S. T. D	56 West 26th "
EDWARD JONES	75 Fifth Avenue.
ROBERT RAY	363 West 28th Street.
GOUVERNEUR M. OGDEN, Treasurer	84 West 11th "
HENRY J. ANDERSON, M. D., LL. D	53 West 36th "
EDWARD L. BEADLE, M. D	Poughkeepsie.
GEORGE T. STRONG	113 East 21st Street.
MANCIUS S. HUTTON, S. T. D	115 Ninth "
HORATIO POTTER, S. T. D., LL. D., D. C. L	38 East 22d "
MARTIN ZBOROWSKI	Morrisania.
JOHN TORREY, M. D , LL. D	Columbia College.
LEWIS M. RUTHERFURD	175 Second Avenue.
THOMAS DE WITT, S. T. D	123 Ninth Street.
JOHN JACOB ASTOR, Jr	338 Fifth Avenue.
JOHN C. JAY, M. D	Rye.
WILLIAM C. SCHERMERHORN	49 West 23d Street.
MORGAN DIX, S. T. D	50 Varick "
FREDERICK A. P. BARNARD, S. T. D., LL. D	Columbia College.
SAMUEL BLATCHFORD, LL. D	12 West 22d Street.
STEPHEN P. NASH	11 West 19th "

COMMITTEES OF THE TRUSTEES.

STANDING COMMITTEE.

NAMES.	RESIDENCES.
GOUVERNEUR M. OGDEN, Chairman	84 West 11th Street.
WILLIAM BETTS, LL. D	122 East 30th "
ROBERT RAY	221 East 28th "
JOHN TORREY, M. D., LL. D	Columbia College.
EDWARD JONES	75 Fifth Avenue.
MARTIN ZBOROWSKI	Morrisania.
LEWIS M. RUTHERFURD	175 Second Avenue.

COMMITTEE ON THE COURSE OF INSTRUCTION.

NAMES.	RESIDENCES.
HORATIO POTTER, S. T. D., LL. D., D. C. L	33 West 24th Street.
MORGAN DIX, S. T. D	50 Varick "
GEORGE T. STRONG	113 East 21st "
LEWIS M. RUTHERFURD	175 Second Avenue.
FREDERICK A. P. BARNARD, S. T. D., LL. D	Columbia College.

COMMITTEE ON THE SCHOOL OF MINES.

NAMES.	RESIDENCES.
WILLIAM BETTS, LL. D., Chairman	122 East 30th Street.
EDWARD JONES	75 Fifth Avenue.
GEORGE T. STRONG	113 East 21st Street.
JOHN TORREY, M. D., LL. D	Columbia College.
LEWIS M. RUTHERFURD	175 Second Avenue.
FREDERICK A. P. BARNARD, S. T. D., LL. D	Columbia College.
HAMILTON FISH, LL. D	134 East 17th Street.

COMMITTEE ON THE SCHOOL OF LAW.

NAMES.	RESIDENCES.
SAMUEL B. RUGGLES, LL. D., Chairman	24 Union Square.
HAMILTON FISH, LL. D.	134 East 17th Street.
GOUVERNEUR M. OGDEN, Esq.	84 West 11th "
GEORGE T. STRONG, Esq.	113 East 21st "
WILLIAM BETTS, LL. D.	122 East 30th "
THEODORE W. DWIGHT, LL. D.	37 Lafayette Place.
STEPHEN P. NASH	11 West 19th Street.

COMMITTEE ON THE LIBRARY.

NAMES.	RESIDENCES.
HENRY J. ANDERSON, M. D., LL. D., Chairman	53 West 36th Street.
GEORGE T. STRONG	113 East 21st "
WILLIAM C. SCHERMERHORN	49 West 23d "
FREDERICK A. P. BARNARD, S. T. D., LL. D.	Columbia College.
BEVERLEY R. BETTS, Clerk	Maspeth, L. I.

COMMITTEE ON HONORS.

NAMES.	RESIDENCES.
WILLIAM BETTS, LL. D., Chairman	122 East 30th Street.
HORATIO POTTER, S. T. D., LL. D., D. C. L.	38 East 22d "
HENRY J. ANDERSON, M. D., LL. D.	53 West 36th "
GEORGE T. STRONG	113 East 21st "
FREDERICK A. P. BARNARD, S. T. D., LL. D.	Columbia College.

RESOLUTION

DIRECTING THE PREPARATION OF A SYNOPSIS

OF THE

RESOLUTIONS OF THE BOARD OF TRUSTEES

OF

COLUMBIA COLLEGE.

Passed November 6, 1865.

1865. Nov. 6. *Resolved*, That the president be requested to prepare a synopsis of the resolutions of the board, exhibiting a history of legislation on all important subjects, and preserving in full all resolutions still in force, to be printed for the use of the board.

Resolved, That a selection from the resolutions of the board, of such as have a relation to the educational objects of the college and its several schools, be printed in connection with the statutes of the college.

RESOLUTIONS

OF THE

TRUSTEES OF COLUMBIA COLLEGE.

ACADEMICAL DRESS.

1788, Aug. 25. A petition from several students of the college was read, setting forth their desire that an order should pass for their wearing gowns; thereupon—

Resolved, That for the present, such of the students as choose to wear gowns, be, and they are hereby, permitted to wear them; and that the board of president and professors ascertain the distinctions between the different classes until the corporation make further regulations on the subject.

1789, April 9. *Resolved*, That the board of president and professors be authorized to require of the students to wear gowns in such cases and under such penalties as they shall judge proper.

827, Jan. 15. A communication from the students on the subject of a regulation adopted by themselves respecting the wearing of caps, having been submitted by the president of the college, requesting the sanction of this board to the same; on motion, resolved that the said communication be referred to the faculty of the college.

1852, Jan. 5. *Resolved*, That in the opinion of this board, the statutes require that the usual prayers should be said in the chapel daily, during the examinations as during the rest of the term, and that the professors should be present at all the examinations, and that long usage requires that the professors and students shall appear at the examination in their gowns.

1854, April 3. The committee of honors made the following report, and its recommendation was adopted :

The committee on honors, to whom was referred certain communications from gentlemen abroad, on the subject of badges of honorary distinctions conferred by the college :

Respectfully report, That they are not able to regard the adoption, by the board, of such badges as expedient ; it is without precedent in any of the numerous literary institutions of our republic, and would seem to conflict with the simplicity of our prevailing tastes and habits. Your committee, however, recommend that the board signify its assent to the public use, on the part of gentlemen residing within the British empire, on whom they may have conferred their higher honorary degrees, of the badges connected with corresponding degrees conferred by the university of Oxford,

Provided that venerable institution shall in comity toward Columbia college, concede to them the privilege.

Respectfully submitted on behalf of the committee.

[Signed] JOHN KNOX.
April 3, 1854.

APPROPRIATIONS, SPECIAL.

1856, July 7. A resolution of this date appropriated the sum of seventy-five dollars, to defray the expenses of a suitable person to be employed in visiting the Michigan university at Ann Arbor, Madison college at Hamilton, and Harvard university at Cambridge, for the purpose of inspecting the astronomical instruments recently purchased for those institutions.

1858, Feb. 1. An appropriation of one hundred dollars was made, to enable the professor of astronomy to purchase maps, charts, models, and printed forms; and also for the repair of astronomical instruments.

APPROPRIATIONS, SPECIAL.

1859, Nov. 7. *Resolved,* That the sum of one thousand dollars be appropriated to the purchase of physical apparatus, to be expended in Europe under the direction of Prof. McCulloh.

1860, May 7. *Resolved,* That the sum of two hundred and fifty dollars be appropriated in aid of the proposed expedition to Labrador, for observing the total solar eclipse to take place on the eighteenth of July next, provided a sufficient sum be raised for that purpose, and in such case that the above amount be paid to Mr. Geo. W. Blunt.

1865, June 5. *Resolved,* That the sum of one thousand dollars be appropriated, to be expended under the direction of the president and professor Peck, for the purchase of the instruments for surveying, &c., recommended in the president's report.

1865, Dec. 18. *Resolved,* That the appropriation of one thousand dollars in June last, for the benefit of the department of mathematics and astronomy, or so much of it as remains unexpended, be applied to the purchase of any apparatus which, in the opinion of the professor, approved by the president, may be most needed for use or illustration in any of the branches taught by the professor in that department.

1867, Oct. 7. *Resolved,* That an extraordinary appropriation be made of two thousand dollars in currency, to be placed in the hands of Dr. Barnard, for the purpose of making such purchases while in Europe for additions to the scientific apparatus and library of the college as he may deem beneficial; and that the treasurer pay the amount on his draft or otherwise.

1867, Nov. 4. Laid over under the ordinance of Nov. 26, 1866, and called up and passed Nov. 4, 1867.

1868, April 6. A resolution appropriating five hundred dollars, to be applied in paying duties and charges upon the objects purchased under the foregoing resolution, was similarly
1868, May 4. laid over to May 4, and adopted.

APPROPRIATIONS, PERMANENT.

1866, June 12. *Resolved,* That until the further order of this board, the following sums be annually appropriated to the purposes named, viz. :

For apparatus and other permanent aids to instruction in physics....................	$600 00
For the same in mechanics, surveying, and astronomy.............................	400 00

to be expended under the direction of the professors giving instruction in those branches, with the approval of the president. For the department of botany, five hundred dollars, to be expended under the direction of Dr. Torrey. As to each of the foregoing appropriations, if unexpended in any year in whole or in part, the balance unexpended to remain to the credit of the department and added to the appropriation of the following year.

For the classical, mathematical, and english departments, three hundred dollars, to be expended under the direction of the professors in said departments, with the approval of the president.

For supplies, thirty-seven hundred dollars. For printing and advertising, twenty-five hundred dollars.

1866, June 12. *Resolved,* That until further order of this board, the following sums be annually appropriated to the purposes named in the school of mines, viz. :

For the department of mineralogy...........	$500
Do. do. geology..............	500
Do. do. metallurgy...........	500
For models, drawings of machines, furnaces, &c......................................	300
For the department of analytical chemistry...	3,500

The same to be expended under the direction of the professors in the departments to which said appropriations belong, with the approval of the president.

For the library $1,000, to be expended under the direction of the library committee.

As to each of the foregoing appropriations, if unexpended any year in whole or in part, the balance unexpended to remain to the credit of the appropriation, and to be added to the appropriation of the following year.

For supplies $2,000.

For printing and advertising $2,000.

1863, March 3. *Resolved*, That, until otherwise ordered, the sum of three hundred dollars for defraying the expenses of the commencement be annually paid by the treasurer on the order of the president at any time within ten days, before the day appointed for the commencement.

1866, Nov. 5. *Resolved*, That the standing annual appropriation of two hundred dollars, heretofore made to the department of physics for contingent expenses, be discontinued after the close of the present year, and that the contingencies of the department be hereafter provided for out of the annual appropriation of six hundred dollars made to the department by resolution of June last.

Resolved, That hereafter, and until the further order of this Board, the sum of three hundred dollars be annually appropriated for the purchase of chemicals, and the purchase and repair of apparatus in the department of general chemistry, the same to be payable within each financial year ending September 30th, and that any former resolution on this subject be, and the same is hereby, repealed.

Resolved, That the foregoing resolution shall apply to the current financial year; and that any bills which may have been incurred by the department, within the limit of the appropriation heretofore made, since January last, be paid by the treasurer.

ATTENDANCE AT PRAYERS.

1844, Nov. 4.   *Resolved*, That the presence of the faculty as well as that of the students, shall be insisted upon at the daily prayers and declamation in the chapel.

BOTANICAL GARDEN.

1851, Jan. 6.   On the 6th of January, 1851, it was resolved that the property of the college should be laid out in building lots, with a space in the centre thereof, to remain open for a park, and that the privilege of placing the college buildings on this space be reserved in the conveyances to purchasers.

Also, that in laying out the college property, a space be reserved for the site of a church.

Also, that as soon as a map of the property shall have been made and approved, copies shall be printed for the use of the college.

1856, Feb. 4.   *Resolved*, That it be referred to the standing committee to report to the board at its next meeting the present condition of the property of the college in the nineteenth ward known as botanic garden, at what time any, and what part thereof may be offered to be leased, and the probable rents to be obtained therefor; to prepare and submit with their report the draft of a lease applicable to said grounds: that the committee at the same time submit a statement of the expenditures already made in preparing said grounds for the occupation of the college buildings, and for being disposed of by lease or otherwise.

1856, Oct. 6.   The standing committee was authorized to contract a loan not exceeding fifty thousand dollars, for the purpose of regulating the property known as the botanic garden, and to give security by bond and mortgage upon such part of the real estate of the college as they may deem proper and sufficient, and on December 6, 1858, it was resolved that it be referred to the standing committee, to consider and report upon the following subjects: What measures are advisable to effect the early leasing of the botanic garden property; the most expedient mode of disposition thereof by leases; the clauses and provisions proper to be inserted in such leases; and in what parcels lots ought to be leased.

<small>1858, Dec. 6.</small>

<small>1859, Jan. 3.</small> The standing committee having reported a map of the botanic garden tract, showing the mode in which it was proposed to subdivide the same for leasing; showing also modes of laying out stable lots; propose that the plan designated for the upper block be adopted for each of the blocks. That the erection of stables on any other part of the property should be prohibited. The stable lots thus shown, to be separately leased (with a right of way through the alley), preference being given to tenants of the college. The committee recommend the approval of this plan, and that a survey of the western line of the property be immediately made, and a map to conform to the same be afterward prepared. They advise leasing by private negotiation rather than by auction, and recommend that leases be granted for four terms of twenty-one years each, with covenants and conditions for the payment of rent, taxes, and assessments; to guard against nuisances, to secure proper improvement within a specified time, to express proper stipulation in regard to renewals, and to reserve courtyards, &c., &c.; and also that leases be granted for stable lots with such provisions inserted as may prevent their being offensive to the occupants of the neighboring lots, preserve private ways, &c.

Also, the following resolutions which were passed:

Resolved, That the recommendations contained in the report of the standing committee, dated January 3, 1859, be approved.

Resolved, That the standing committee have full power to prepare and have printed such blank leases as they may think most conducive to the interests of the college, and to make the same known as comprising in detail the provisions which will be inserted in the leases of lots situate in the botanic garden tract; and also, power to take such other steps as they may deem expedient to effect the early leasing of the above-mentioned property, and to conclude agreements with persons for leases of the same in lots.

1859, May 2. *Resolved*, That the standing committee have power to direct the execution on the part of the college of all such leases of lots in the botanic garden tract as they may conclude agreements for under the resolutions of the trustees passed the 3d of January, 1859; and that the clerk be authorized to affix the seal of this corporation to such leases, under the direction of the standing committee.

1859, Nov. 7. *Resolved*, That the sum of thirty dollars be appropriated for preserving the college grounds in the botanic garden from washing; and that a sum not exceeding four hundred dollars be appropriated for planting trees in and around the reserved square; and that the above sums be expended under the direction of the standing committee.

ERECTION OF COLLEGE BUILDINGS.

1854, July 10. A resolution was passed, authorizing the payment of one hundred dollars for each of the presented plans of the college buildings proposed to be erected, and to deposit such plans in the college library.

1855, April 5. The standing committee were on this day ordered by resolution to report on the practicability and expediency of obtaining in some central situation temporary accommodations for college purposes, in event of an early disposition of the property on the north side of the new street.

1857, Feb. 6. A resolution passed on this date, ordered that the standing committee should examine the property of this college at the old botanic garden, with a view to designate a site for the erection of the college buildings, and to procure designs for the same.

COLLEGE BUILDING, SITE FOR.

1866, March 5. *Resolved*, That a special committee be appointed to inquire into the expediency of procuring land for the permanent occupation of the college and its several schools, and that they report to this board at its next meeting.

This committee reported April 2, but the report led to no action.

COLLEGE BUILDINGS, USE OF.

1859, Feb. 7. A communication having been read from the trustees of the Bloomingdale presbyterian church, requesting the use of the college chapel for religious services, it was

Resolved, That it is the opinion of this board that the college buildings should not be used for other than academical purposes, and that it is inexpedient to comply with the request.

CATALOGUE.

1851, March 3. A resolution of this date authorized the president to prepare a complete catalogue of the college, and print one thousand copies of the same.

1859 Feb. 7. This resolution was not acted on, and on February 7, 1859, it was further resolved, that the president be authorized to publish a general catalogue of the alumni of this college, from its establishment; with such authentic notes of the subsequent life and career of each alumnus as he may, with the assistance of the alumni, be able to procure.

This also remained without effect.

1864, Nov. 7 *Resolved,* That a full catalogue of King's and Columbia college, comprehending the governors, professors, trustees and alumni, with the degrees conferred, be published under the direction of the president.

This resolution was acted upon immediately, and the catalogue was published in the following year.

The following relate to the annual catalogue:

1860, Oct. 1. *Resolved,* That the list of the faculty and students of the law school and of the medical school be included in the catalogue of Columbia college.

1861, May 20. *Resolved,* That $250 be annually appropriated for printing a catalogue under the direction of a committee, to be issued on or before January 1st in each year.

1864, Nov. 7. *Resolved,* That in the annual catalogue of the college the names of the students in the several classes be printed in alphabetic order, those of the five students who have received honors being prefixed to each roll; and that at the close of each session a list of each class—the names in the order of merit—be printed, and that a copy be presented to each student, and another to his parents or guardian.

The provisions of this resolution are practically annulled by those embodied in chapter X of the revised statutes of 1865.

CHEMISTRY, DEPARTMENT OF.

1857, Dec. 7.   Mr. Ruggles, Dr. Torrey, and Mr. Jones having been appointed a special committee, were instructed to report whether in their opinion the voluntary mode as practised by professor Joy, should be subject to any regulations.

1858, Jan. 4.   On January 4, 1858, it was resolved, that more time should be given in the instruction in chemistry to a portion of the senior class; that at least thirty-six lectures on mineralogy, geology, and physiology, and, if necessary, further instruction in chemistry, be given to the students of the school of science; that $250 be allowed the professor of chemistry for the services of his assistant, from October 1, 1857, to March 1, 1858, and $200 per annum be allowed for the wages of a servant in the laboratory; that $500 be expended in the purchase of a chemical cabinet; that the mineralogical and geological collections be rearranged and newly labelled; and that the same committee who reported the resolutions be appointed to carry them out, and

Resolved, That $300 yearly be paid to the professor of chemistry, on his presenting proper vouchers, for materials and perishable apparatus used in the lectures and laboratory, to commence on the 1st January, 1858.

1860, Feb. 6.   *Resolved,* That the annual appropriation of three hundred dollars for the department of chemistry, shall be applied to the contingent expenses of that department; and any balance thereof, not necessary in any year for that purpose, may be expended for the purchase of apparatus.

1861, June 3.   On the 3d of June, 1861, it was decided that the department of practical chemistry should be discontinued, and that the instruction in chemistry to the under-graduates should only consist of lectures and recitations with the usual illustrations.

CHEMISTRY, DEPARTMENT OF.

1861, Dec. 2.   A communication having been received from professor Joy, asking permission to establish a working laboratory in the city at his own expense, to give instruction at hours not interfering with his college duties, the following resolution was introduced, but failed for want of a quorum:

Resolved, That the board is desirous of availing itself of the liberal offer of professor Joy; and that a committee be appointed to confer with him, having in view the carrying into successful operation of the establishment proposed by him, or such other as may be deemed expedient.

This resolution was never revived; but, two months later, the subject was disposed of by the passage of the following resolution:

1862, Feb. 3.   *Resolved,* That during the pleasure of the trustees the professor of chemistry shall be at liberty to deliver instruction in analytical chemistry at the laboratory of the college, under the following regulations:

1. That under-graduates and persons of good moral character may practise in the laboratory two hours *per diem.*

2. All such students shall pay at the rate of not more than $300 per year. At the beginning of the term each student shall deposit with the professor $30, from which at the end of the term shall be deducted the cost of materials consumed, and apparatus broken or injured, and the remainder returned to the student. Out of this sum shall be paid all expenses peculiar to the working laboratory, as lights, fuel, &c.

3. At the close of each college term the professor shall report to the treasurer:

First—The names of all students who have attended, specifying the under-graduates.

Second—All sums received for tuition and as deposits, specifying the sums paid by each student and the balance of deposit due him.

CHEMISTRY, DEPARTMENT OF.

Third—All sums paid for the working laboratory;—the receipts being in excess of such expenditure, the balance to be paid over to the treasurer, to be used for the benefit of the chemical department.

4. The treasurer shall pay annually one hundred dollars to the professor for gas and charcoal used in the chemical department; such part thereof as shall be used in the working laboratory to be included in the report required as above, and such expense no longer to be paid as part of the cost of the general supplies of the college.

1863, March 2. On March 2, 1863, it was resolved that $200, directed in resolution of January 4, 1858, to be paid to the servant of the professor of chemistry, be paid to the professor or such person as he may designate.

1863, Dec. 21. On December 21, 1863, the resolution of February 3, 1862, was amended to read "academic year" for "term" and the "president" instead of the "treasurer," as the officer to whom such report shall be made.

1865, May 23. *Resolved*, That the treasurer be directed to pay two hundred dollars out of the fund deposited with him for the benefit of the chemical department, as compensation for services rendered in said department by Henry B. Cornwall, as assistant; and also to pay professor Joy the remaining balance of said fund, viz.: three hundred dollars, to be expended by him for apparatus and chemicals for the use of the department during his visit to Europe.

1865, Oct. 9. *Resolved*, That the standing appropriation of two hundred dollars per annum to the department of chemistry, for attendance on the laboratory, be applied only to the payment of the wages of a servant, and be paid monthly by the treasurer directly to such servant, during the time of his employment.

Resolved, further, That the professor of general chemistry be authorized to employ a skilled assistant in his laboratory, whose duty shall be, not only to aid him in the business of his department, but also to keep the meteorological record for the college and the regents of the university, at an annual salary of five hundred dollars, to be paid on the usual college quarter days.

1865, Dec. 18. *Resolved*, That the appropriation of two hundred dollars per annum for the wages of a servant of the professor of general chemistry, be hereafter paid to such professor upon the production by him of vouchers, showing the previous payments by him of such wages.

1866, Jan. 2. *Resolved*, That the recommendation of the committee (to whom was referred a petition of the senior class for time for excursions), that on such days, not exceeding four in each academic year, when the last hour of the senior class shall be occupied with chemistry or geology, such hour may be employed by them with the consent of the president, on such excursions as may be advised and superintended by the professor of chemistry, be adopted.

CHURCH SITE, LOTS RESERVED FOR.

1859, June 22. The action of the standing committee in regard to the application for lots for churches, and their recommendation that twelve lots, viz.: lots 173 to 178, inclusive, and 199 to 204, inclusive, fronting on Fiftieth and Fifty-first streets, be reserved for the erection of a protestant episcopal church, to cost not less than eighty thousand dollars, was approved.

1867, April 1. *Whereas*, A long period has elapsed since the resolution was passed in June, 1859, reserving certain lots for the site of a church; and it being now represented that there was no probability that any application would be made for the reserved lots on Fiftieth and Fifty-first streets for the foregoing purpose, therefore

Resolved, In conformity with the recommendation of the standing committee, that they have power to lease the above lots upon such terms as they shall judge expedient, and to direct the seal of the college to be affixed to any leases that may be granted under this resolution.

CLOAK-ROOM.

1867, Jan. 7. *Resolved,* That the president be required to see that hooks be provided in all the recitation and lecture rooms not already so furnished, for the hanging of cloaks and overcoats against the wall; and that such students as find themselves encumbered with those garments in their seats be allowed to avail themselves of such conveniences for disposing of them.

Resolved, further, That the cloak-room be continued as heretofore, and that, during the hours of chapel and scholastic exercises, garments, books, or other property may be deposited there in charge of the janitor; but that, whilst all care and vigilance shall be exercised to guard such property against depredations, the college cannot undertake to insure it, or to be responsible for damages in case of loss.

COMMENCEMENTS AND EXHIBITIONS.

1821, June 4. On June 4, 1821, it was resolved that commencements in future should take place between the hours of
1825, May 2. nine and three; on May 2, 1825, that the standing committee and the faculty unite in enforcing more rigor-
1842, Aug. 1. ous discipline at commencement; and on August 1, 1842, that the arrangements for commencements be superintended by the president and a committee of the trus-
1842, Dec. 5. tees. On December 5, 1842, a resolution was adopted,

providing, by the addition of a section to the twelfth chapter of the statutes, that a committee of trustees to be *annually* appointed, should make, with the president, all necessary arrangements for commencements; and that all expenses for the same, not exceeding two hundred dollars, should be defrayed by the college.

1844, Nov. 4. In 1844 it had been resolved that public exhibitions should be held in May and December, and that the faculty and not less than four trustees, be required to be present;

1851, June 14. but on June 14, 1851, it was resolved that the semi-annual exhibitions and the award of prizes for excellence in exercises in declamation be discontinued.

1863, Mar. 2. The permanent provision for defraying the expenses attending the commencement celebration was increased to three hundred dollars per annum, payable on the order of the president at any time within ten days before the day appointed for commencement.

1855, Feb. 5. A communication was received from the Philolexian society, containing a request " that the privilege be delegated to the Philolexian society, of electing from their number one speaker to represent them at the semi-annual exhibition of each collegiate year." "That members of the senior and junior classes alone be eligible to the speakership; and that the essay be in all cases subject to the approval of the president of the college."

The request was granted.

1856, Feb. 4. A communication having been received from the Columbian Peithologian society, containing a request that the privilege of nominating a speaker at the semi-annual exhibition, similar to that granted to the Philolexian society, on Feb. 5, 1855, be likewise allowed to to them; it was

Resolved, That the request be granted; that members of the senior and junior classes alone be eligible to the speakership; and that the essay be first subjected to the president for approval.

DIPLOMAS.

1826, Jan. 2.   It was resolved, January 2, 1826, that the expense of honorary degrees be defrayed by the trustees.

Until the year 1830, honorary degrees appear not to have been always attested by the issuing of formal diplomas. On the 19th of July in that year, the following resolution was placed upon the minutes:

1830, July 19.   *Resolved*, That the faculty do prepare the proper diplomas for the honorary degrees to be hereafter conferred; and that the faculty do also prepare the proper diplomas for the honorary degrees conferred during the last seven years, and for which diplomas have not yet been given, stating the time when the said degrees were conferred; and that the clerk of the board affix, or cause to be affixed, the seal of the college to all the diplomas above mentioned; that no fees be charged for such diplomas, but that the actual expense thereof be paid by the treasurer.

1831, June 7.   It was once more resolved that the diplomas for the honorary degrees directed to be prepared by the faculty by a former resolution of this board, be attested by the corporate seal of the college, and signed by the clerk.

1852, May 2.   It was resolved that all diplomas should be delivered free of all expenses, except the usual fee of eight dollars to the president, and that such fee, and all arrears of dues, must be paid before the delivery of the diploma; and that the seal of the college be affixed to the diplomas, and the use of the engraved plate be allowed to the graduate without charge.

1862, May 19.   It was resolved that each candidate for the degree of master of arts pay a fee of ten dollars.

It does not appear from the minutes at what time the diploma fee was withdrawn from the president and ordered to be paid into the treasury. It appears from the statutes, as published in 1851, that, down to that time, the president continued to receive the fee; but he had ceased to do so before the passage of the following:

1865, March 6. *Resolved,* That all regulations heretofore passed in regard to fees for diplomas be repealed.

Resolved, That no diploma for a degree in course, conferred for proficiency in any department of instruction, be delivered until a fee of five dollars shall be paid for preparing the same; provided, however, that such fee shall not be required from any graduate of the law school, or of the school of mines, who shall have entered therein prior to the passage of this resolution.

ELOCUTION, INSTRUCTION IN.

1844, Nov. 4. *Resolved,* That a professor of elocution be appointed, to hold his office during the pleasure of the board, who shall attend the Freshman class at the expense of the college, such expense not to exceed $200 per annum, and such pupils from the other classes as may be willing to pay for his instruction. But such professor shall not be a member of the board.

Resolved, That in addition to the exercises in declamation directed by the second section of the tenth chapter of the statute to be delivered at the distribution of testimonials, on the first Monday in March, other public exhibitions shall be held in the evenings of the second Monday of May and December, at which the faculty and a number of the trustees, not less than four, shall always be present.

1845, Jan. 14. Under the foregoing resolutions, prof. J. W. S. Hows was appointed professor of elocution, his appointment to take effect from the 9th December, 1844.

1852, Oct. 4. *Resolved,* That it be referred to the president and the faculty to inquire into the practicability of having the professor of elocution drill all the classes of the college at least one hour every day in the practice of elocution.

1853, Feb. 7. The president reported for himself and the faculty under the foregoing resolution, that increased attention to elocution appeared to them to be desirable, but that the object could not be conveniently accomplished during the current year, the distribution of studies having been already made.

1857, Nov. 9. *Resolved,* That the office of professor of elocution be abolished.

For two or three years after this there appears to have been no regular provision made for instruction in elocution. In 1860, the subject was again brought to the attention of the trustees, as follows:

1860, Oct. 1. A communication was received from the board of the college suggesting the expediency of employing an instructor in elocution. This was referred to a special committee, which, at the next succeeding meeting, reported the following resolutions:

1860, Nov. 5. *Resolved,* That it is expedient that instruction in elocution should be afforded to the students of the college; and that two hours in each week should be devoted to that purpose by the instructor.

Resolved, That an instructor in elocution be appointed to hold his office during the current academic year, at the rate of   per annum, to take effect from the time at which he shall commence his duties.

Another resolution was reported, of which the consideration was postponed; but on the 3d of December it was called up and passed in the following words:

1860, Dec. 3. *Resolved,* That the president be authorized to make arrangements for instruction in elocution, so as not to interfere with the regular course of study : merit marks to be given in this department as well as in others.

1862, May 19. Whether any immediate effect was given to this provision does not appear; but on the 19th of May, 1862, a communication was received from Mr. George Vandenhoff, offering his services as an instructor in elocution in college and in the law school, which was referred to the president and faculty of the college, and the professor of municipal law, with power.

1862, June 2. The president reported that Mr. Vandenhoff had been engaged to give instruction in elocution to members of the senior class in college, and to students of the law school, his remuneration to be derived from fees paid by such as should volunteer to be his pupils.

What success attended this arrangement is not recorded.

EXAMINATIONS.

1833, May 3. *Resolved*, That a committee of visitation of not less than six members of the board of trustees, be appointed semi-annually, to attend examinations, and to report to the board after each examination.

1839. In 1839 the number of this committee was increased to twelve, and it was resolved that three of the committee should always be present at the examination of each class.

1851, June 2. *Resolved :* 1st. That the board of trustees be divided into two permanent committees, as follows, viz. :

First Class.	*Second Class.*
CLEMENT C. MOORE,	REV. GARDINER SPRING,
WILLIAM BARD,	REV. JOHN KNOX,
BEVERLEY ROBINSON,	SAMUEL B. RUGGLES,
REV. WM. BERRIAN,	THOMAS L. WELLS,
OGDEN HOFFMAN,	WILLIAM BETTS,
REV. BENJ. I. HAIGHT,	EDWARD JONES,

WM. H. HARRISON,   DR. WM. H. HOBART,
GERRIT G. VAN WAGENEN, JOHN L. MASON,
HAMILTON FISH.   GOUVERNEUR M. OGDEN,
                        ROBERT RAY.

2d. Said committees to attend the summer examinations alternately and the winter examinations alternately.

3d. The committee whose turn it is to attend, to be notified by the president at least three weeks before the examination, and thereupon to meet and appoint a chairman, who shall not twice in succession be the same person, and add to their number twelve of the alumni of the college.

4th. The committee thus constituted to be divided by the chairman into four sections, with a chairman for each. One of the sections to attend the examinations of each class, who shall keep minutes of their attendance, and report the same together with their opinion of the examinations in the several departments to the general committee. From these several reports the general committee shall draw up their report to be presented to the trustees at their next ensuing meeting.

1868, Jan. 6. *Resolved*, That it be referred to a committee to inquire and report on the expediency of abolishing the intermediate examination, and that the committee consist of five members.

The president, and Messrs. Schermerhorn, Blatchford, Haight, and Rutherford were appointed as this committee.

FEES.

1828, April 1. *Resolved*, That the students' fees shall be paid at the time of matriculation; and it shall be the duty of the president to report the names of all students who shall not have paid within thirty days after matriculation.

FEES.

1842, Dec. 5. A resolution reported by the standing committee, provided that in case any student should be transferred from one class to another of higher grade, he should be required to pay an additional half year's tuition fee.

1851, June 15.
1861, June 24. On June 15 a resolution was passed reducing the tuition fee to fifty dollars per annum. On June 24, 1861, it was resolved, that after the termination of that academic year, each graduate, before receiving his diploma, should pay to the treasurer the sum of *ten* dollars; and, also, that each student, on matriculation, should pay a matriculation fee of ten dollars. This **1862, May 19.** was abolished May 19, 1862, when it was resolved, that the annual tuition fees of each student shall be one hundred dollars, and that the payment of a matriculation fee shall be dispensed with. Further, that each candidate for the degree of master of arts in course, shall pay a fee of ten dollars.

1865, March 5. On March 5, 1865, the diploma fee was reduced to five dollars, and made uniform for all degrees.

1865, Jan. 9. *Resolved,* That when a student shall be admitted after the commencement of the scholastic exercises of the year, he shall be required to pay such part of the tuition fee for the year as may be proportional to the time of tuition yet unexpired, provided that no deduction shall be made unless the time of admission be more than two months from the beginning; and that in estimating the amount to be paid, fractions of months be counted as entire months.

1865, April 3. *Resolved,* That whenever it shall appear to the satisfaction of the president and treasurer, that a student who is of good moral character and industrious habits, is unable to pay his fee for tuition, such student may be permitted to proceed without charge; or, in case he shall so elect, he may give his note for the amount, payable at his convenience, after graduation.

1865, Oct. 9. *Resolved,* That in the case of industrious, meritorious, and promising young men who may be desirous of attending the course of instruction in the school of mines without being able to pay the necessary fee for tuition, the president and treasurer be authorized to use the same discretion in admitting such students as they are now empowered to exercise in regard to undergraduate students.

1866, May 7. *Resolved,* That hereafter the annual tuition fees in the school of mines, shall be, for students who take the regular course, or a special course of analytical chemistry, or of assaying, and for candidates for such degrees as the trustees of the college may establish, two hundred dollars; for students who pursue only certain branches of study, the charges shall be made proportional to the time devoted to them and to the expense attendant on the conduct of such course.

FINANCIAL POLICY, PERMANENT.

1861, June 3. *Resolved,* That it be referred to a special committee of five members of this board, of whom the chairman shall be one, to consider and report such measures as, if adopted, after the present financial year shall reduce the annual expenditure of the institution to the amount of its available income.

1861, June 24. At a subsequent meeting, the committee here provided for reported resolutions, which were adopted, reducing the salaries of the president, professors, and other officers of the college, and also the annual appropriation for the law library, and for printing and advertising for the law school; abolishing the semi-annual exhibition, and the prizes previously awarded for excellence in declamation; indefinitely postponing the appointment of tutors, contemplated by resolution of Nov. 5, 1860; and requiring a matriculation fee from each matriculating student, and a diploma fee from each graduating student, of ten dollars.

1865, Nov. 6. *Resolved,* That it be referred to a special committee to consider and report what annual expenditure ought to be estimated for as necessary to sustain in due efficiency the departments and schools of instruction now organized, and what disposition ought to be made of so much of the income of the college from time to time to be realized, as may not be required for that purpose; and also to inquire and report as to the expediency of limiting the annual expenditure, and of creating an accumulating fund from surplus income, to be applied to the payment of the present debt and of assessments, and to defray the cost of buildings which it may be hereafter expedient to erect; and also to make such recommendations as they may think proper, relative to the adoption of a permanent policy for the management of the finances of the institution.

Mr. Ogden, Mr. Bradford, the Rev. Dr. Dix, Mr. Jones, Mr. Rutherfurd, and the president, were appointed the committee.

1866, Nov. 26. The following ordinance reported by the committee appointed November 6, 1865, to consider the expediency of fixing a permanent financial policy was adopted:

ORDINANCE ESTABLISHING A PERMANENT FINANCIAL POLICY.

Whereas, In view of the propriety of extinguishing as early as possible the present indebtedness of the college, of meeting probable assessments for city improvements, and of providing for the college and its schools, buildings more convenient than those occupied by them at present, and better adapted to promote their educational objects, it is expedient that the annual expenditures be kept within such reasonable limits as, while insuring a liberal support to the departments and schools of instruction at present existing, shall leave a surplus for the accumulation of a fund to be applied to the important objects above mentioned; therefore, be it ordained, by the trustees of Columbia college, as follows:

FINANCIAL POLICY, PERMANENT.

ARTICLE I.—The surplus income of the college, which shall remain after the payment of the annual expenditures, shall be annually appropriated and set apart for an accumulating and sinking fund. The said annual expenditures shall only be made for the several purposes hereinafter set forth, and shall not exceed the sums hereinafter named for such purposes : *Provided,* That this rule shall not apply to salaries, nor prevent the creation of any new professorship or other office which the interests of the college may demand ; nor prevent the expenditure of the proceeds of sale of any real estate in the acquisition or improvement of any other real estate or buildings in their place.

EXPENDITURES FOR THE ACADEMIC DEPARTMENT.

Departments of instruction :
- Of physics......... $700
- " chemistry....... 500
- " mechanics and astronomy.... 700
- " geodesy and surveying........ 500
- Botanical collection. 700
- Library............ 3,000

As to each of these items, if the appropriation made in any year be not expended, in whole or in part, the balance unexpended may be added to the appropriation of the succeeding year.

Classical, English, and mathematical departments.	$500
Prizes	150
College societies	700
Supplies	3,700
Printing and advertising.......................	2,500
Commencement and exhibitions................	500
Scholarships and fellowships	5,500
Contingencies.....	5,000

Insurance, whatever may be necessary.
Repairs, whatever may be necessary.

TREASURER'S OFFICE.

Expenses of office............................ 250

CLERK'S OFFICE.

Expenses of office $150

EXPENDITURES FOR THE SCHOOL OF MINES.

Departments of instruction:
Of mineralogy...... $750
" geology 750
" palæontology*... 750
" metallurgy...... 750
" metallurgic laboratory....... 500
" chemistry....... 4,000
" mining engineering........... 750
" drawing 500
" civil engineering. 750
Library 2,000

As to each of these items, if the appropriation made in any year be not expended, in whole or in part, the balance unexpended may be added to the appropriation of the succeeding year.

Supplies $3,500
Printing and advertising 2,500
Repairs, enlargement, alteration, and improvement of building, furniture, and fixtures, whatever may be necessary.
Contingencies. 1,500
Prizes 700

EXPENDITURES FOR THE SCHOOL OF LAW.

Rent, whatever may be necessary.
Library 1,000
Supplies 1,500
Prizes 700
Commencement 250
Printing and advertising........................ 750
Repairs, whatever may be necessary.
Contingencies. 1,000

---

* This title inserted by an amendment adopted May 4, 1867.

MISCELLANEOUS EXPENDITURES.

Real estate, whatever may be necessary.
Interest, whatever may be necessary.
Taxes, whatever may be necessary.

Furniture for the president's house ......$250 } If the appropriation in any year be not expended, the balance unexpended may be added to the appropriation of the succeeding year.

Provided, however, That nothing herein contained shall be taken to affect the regulations for the support of the law school, heretofore adopted.

ARTICLE II.—Said surplus shall be invested and accumulated, under the direction of the treasurer, the chairman of the board of trustees, and the president of the college, in the name of the college, on bond and mortgage on improved and unincumbered real estate in the city of New York, or in stocks of the United States, or of the state of New York, or of the city of New York; and all interest received thereon, from time to time, shall be so invested. But such surplus or interest may be temporarily invested, under their direction, by deposit in the New York life insurance and trust company or the United States trust company, or by temporary loan to the United States, or in the United States treasury notes or certificates of indebtedness.

ARTICLE III.—The said officers above named shall be styled managers of the accumulating fund. They shall keep minutes of their proceedings; and they shall report the same at every meeting of the board of trustees, and shall annually report the condition and amount of said fund, its modes of investment and other matters connected therewith.

ARTICLE IV.—The said fund may be applied from time to time, under the direction of the board of trustees, to the payment of the debt of the college, or of assessments upon its estate imposed by law; or to defray other charges upon its estate, or the cost of the erection of buildings or acquisition of land; but shall be applied to no other purpose until such fund shall amount to five hundred thousand dollars.

ARTICLE V.—This ordinance shall not be altered, amended, or repealed, nor shall any appropriation be made in contravention thereof, without a vote of a majority of the members present, nor unless the proposed alteration, amendment, repeal, or appropriation shall have been presented at a previous meeting, and approved by a majority of the members present at such previous meeting.

ARTICLE VI.—This ordinance shall take effect from and after the first Tuesday of March, 1867.

FREE TUITION.

1868, April 6. *Resolved*, That the president be authorized to make publication in such form as he may deem expedient, of the liberal terms on which students are received in Columbia college, and into the school of law, and the school of mines, distinctly stating that instruction is given free of all charge for tuition to every deserving candidate who may apply, and whose circumstances will not enable him to pay the regular fees.

GEBHARD FUND.

1843, April 3. A communication, dated February 4, 1843, was received from the executors of Frederic Gebhard, deceased, stating that the said Frederic Gebhard had bequeathed to the college the sum of twenty thousand dollars, for the purpose of founding a professorship of the german language and literature, and proposing to pay over the same on or after the 30th day of March next ensuing. Whereupon the board resolved "with a high sense of the liberality of the donor," to accept the bequest on the conditions proposed.

GRAMMAR SCHOOL.

They further resolved that the professorship to be established should be styled the "Gebhard professorship of german language and literature;" and further, that the treasurer, with the advice and approval of the standing committee, invest as a distinct fund, the bequest of the late Frederic Gebhard.

1862, April 7. *Resolved*, That the eleven thousand dollars, part of the Gebhard fund expected to be paid in, be invested in the bond of Thomas Slocomb for fifty-five thousand four hundred dollars ($55,400), and in mortgages by which the same is secured; and that such securities to the extent of the said eleven thousand dollars ($11,000), be held as a separate investment of so much of the Gebhard fund; and that the treasurer pay to the Gebhard professor, interest on the last mentioned sum at the rate of six per cent. per annum, quarterly on the first day of each of the months of January, April, July and October, in each and every year; the balance of the interest to be derived from the investment to be applied to the payment of taxes on the fund.

1862, Nov. 3. *Resolved*, That eleven thousand dollars, part of the Gebhard fund, lately invested in the bond and mortgages of Thomas Slocomb, which were paid on the 1st November, 1862, be re-invested in the bond and mortgage of the Dutch church for twenty thousand dollars as of that date; and that such securities, to the extent of eleven thousand dollars, be held as a separate investment of so much of the Gebhard fund; also resolved that the Gebhard fund shall be entitled to priority of payment out of the said securities.

1862, May 19. On recommendation of the standing committee it was ordered that the separate bank account of the Gebhard fund be discontinued.

GRAMMAR SCHOOL.

1827, Dec. 3. It was resolved in 1827 that a grammar school should be established under the patronage of the trustees, that the name of the school should be "The grammar school of Columbia college," and that the board of trustees should superintend it.

The following were the rules adopted for the organization and government of the school :

There shall be a master and such assistants as may be thought necessary. The regular branches of english shall be taught, and so much at least of the classics and mathematics as shall be equal to the requirements of a student qualified to enter the freshman class of Columbia college. The board of the college may appoint and dismiss at pleasure the master and assistants, and define the duties and make all the necessary by-laws for the government of the school, and report the state of the school annually to the trustees. The expenses of the school shall be defrayed from the moneys received for tuition, and the trustees do not engage to make good deficiencies. On the other hand the whole of these moneys shall be appropriated to the support of the school. And further,

Resolved, That this plan shall not go into operation until it is ascertained that forty scholars will be sent to the school, and will pay at the rate of twelve dollars and fifty cents quarter-yearly; and as soon as that shall be ascertained, the board of the college may hire a house or rooms for the purpose, and proceed to organize the school.

That the trustees may discontinue the school if they shall think it disadvantageous or useless to the college, and make such alterations as they may deem advisable. And that every school, from which shall be admitted in any one year into the college five students, shall have the privilege of sending one scholar who shall be gratuitously educated by the college.

1828, Feb. 4. In 1828 this last resolution was so amended as to make the price of tuition not more than fifteen dollars, quarter-yearly, instead of twelve dollars and fifty cents.

1828, April 17. On April 17, 1828, the board of the college were authorized to open a grammar school, appoint a teacher, and hire a house or apartments for the purpose. It was also ordered that such teacher shall be allowed the moneys paid for tuition fees, after deducting rent and necessary expenses, and that if the surplus, after making the deductions, do not amount to five hundred dollars during the first year, the trustees will make it up to that sum; also that the school shall be conducted, in all respects, according to the plan heretofore adopted, and that the foregoing resolutions be in force for one year and no longer; that should the school be continued after the year, the trustees will make such disposition of the tuition fees as may appear to be most beneficial to the school and the college; and that the fee be twelve dollars and fifty cents quarter-yearly.

Such of the resolutions passed in 1827 as are inconsistent with those passed at this time were repealed.

1830, Dec. 7.   A resolution of the board constituted a committee to superintend and control the grammar school in so far as not to interfere with the superintendence of the faculty, and ordered that a semi-annual report should be made to the board.

1831, Oct. 31.   An elaborate report on the condition and prospects of the grammar school was presented by the committee on the same, concluding with a resolution, which was adopted, appointing professor Anthon rector of the school, at a salary of two thousand two hundred dollars; the resolution further providing, that should the net proceeds of the school not amount to that sum, the rector should receive said net proceeds in lieu thereof.

1831, Dec. 5.   In December, 1831, it was ordered that all disbursements for the school should be made under the direction of this committee and be paid on their certificate by the treasurer of the college.

1833, May 1.   At a meeting of the trustees of Columbia college on this date, the following was submitted by the committee on the grammar school:

"Memorandum of agreement (subject to the approbation of the trustees) between professor Anthon and the chairman of the grammar school committee:

"1. On the 1st of May, instant, professor Anthon agrees to take the grammar school into his own hands for his own account.

"2. He shall defray all the expenses thereof, of all sorts, including repairs of building, &c., so that the college is not to be called on in any way to bear any charges therefor, it being, however, expressly understood that professor Anthon is not to defray any expenses occasioned by damages done by fire or inevitable accident.

"3. He will pay for the current year to end December 31, a rent at the rate of eight hundred dollars per annum. From and after January 1, 1834, the rent shall be one thousand dollars per annum, payable quarterly.

"4. The arrears of rent, if any, and all sums advanced by the treasurer of the college for the school, are to be paid in installments with all convenient speed, and the whole amour t at present due to the college by the school is to be fully paid up by the 1st of January, 1834, the college being allowed the usual rate of interest on said sum or balance until that day.

"5. The guarantee by the college to Mr. Shea for the payment of his salary to cease forthwith.*

"6. All the outstanding credits of the school to be assigned to, and all the outstanding debts of the school to be liquidated by professor Anthon.

"7. The rent stipulated for above from the 1st of January, 1834, to be neither increased nor diminished while professor Anthon holds the school.

"8. The arrangement herein made is to have no bearing whatever on professor Anthon's salary as a professor of the college, and is entirely distinct therefrom.

"9. This agreement not to interfere with the super-

---

* The arrangement here spoken of was made November 23, 1830, and guaranteed Mr. Shea a salary of $1,750 per annum.

vision which may be exercised over the school by the trustees or by their authority.

"10. This agreement shall not be rescinded until three months' notice shall have been given by one of the parties to the other." Whereupon,

Resolved, That the committee on the grammar school be authorized to execute an agreement with professor Anthon on the foregoing terms.

1842, Feb. 21. In 1842, it was resolved, that the regents of the university and superintendent of common schools be informed by the committee that all persons who desire it will be instructed as common-school teachers in the grammar school of Columbia college, in the manner and pursuant to the instruction and direction of the regents and the superintendent.

1864, Feb. 1. *Resolved*, That the notice called for under the agreement of May 1, 1833, between the trustees and the late rector of the grammar school, be given by the former to the latter, and that the said agreement be rescinded from and after three months' service of a notice to that effect on the Jay professor, and on the party or parties now in charge of the school.

In consequence of this notice, the grammar ceased to exist as a branch of the college in the spring of 1864.

GREENWOOD CEMETERY.

A burial lot having been tendered to the college by the president of the Greenwood cemetery, it was

1841, March 1. *Resolved*, That the offer be accepted, and that the clerk of this board be instructed to address a respectful answer to the president, stating such acceptance, and returning the thanks of this board for the liberal gift of the said cemetery. The standing committee was charged with the selection of the lot.

1846, Dec. 15. *Resolved,* That the committee be discharged of the duty of selecting the lot granted to the college by the trustees of Greenwood cemetery, and that the president, as soon as may be convenient, make selection of the same and report to this board.

1847, March 23. *Resolved,* That the president be empowered to cause the lot of ground assigned to the college by the Greenwood cemetery to be enclosed within a quickset or other living hedge, and otherwise suitably arranged, provided that the cost to the college shall not exceed the sum of twenty dollars.

1858, Oct. 27. In relation to the subject of burials in the ground in Greenwood cemetery, belonging to the college, which had been referred to the standing committee, it was

Resolved, To recommend to the trustees that interments, in the case of the death of any of the faculty or students of the college, be allowed, under a written order from the president, or in his absence from the senior professor present.

HERBARIUM.

1860, Nov. 5. A communication was received from Dr. Torrey, offering to the college his entire botanical collection and botanical library, in consideration of being permitted to occupy, for five years, a dwelling on the college green, free of rent. Dr. Torrey also proposed, in case a curator were appointed to take care of the collection, to deliver lectures on botany in its various departments, and to give instruction in the use of the microscope, to the students of the college.

The herbarium was stated to embrace forty thousand species; and the annual increase to be from two to four thousand, of all which he proposed that the college should have the benefit. It was further stated to contain original specimens of all the plants described by Torrey and Gray in the Flora of North America, of nearly all those of the collections made by the United States and by the several state governments since 1818, and those obtained in the expeditions to Panama, as well as those gathered by professor Holton in New Granada. Besides these, it was said to embrace also most of the illustrations of the arctic flora gathered by the British polar expeditions, and a large number of specimens from the botanists of the East Indies, received through the British East India Company. And in addition to all these it was said further to contain large contributions from most of the eminent botanists of England, Scotland, and the continent of Europe, with many plants from the Museum of Natural History in Paris, the Imperial Academy at St. Petersburg, and the Imperial Society at Moscow.

The library was stated to contain six hundred volumes, many of them rare and costly works, now obtainable only with great difficulty.

The communication having been read, the following resolutions were introduced and passed:

Resolved, That the proposition of Dr. Torrey be accepted, and that it be referred to a special committee to acknowledge the donation and arrange the necessary details.

Resolved, That the thanks of this board be returned to Dr. Torrey for his liberal donation, and his enlightened consideration of the highest interest of the college; and that a copy of these resolutions be furnished to him.

CURATOR FOR THE BOTANICAL COLLECTION.

1861, Dec. 16. *Resolved*, That the bills [for the removal and arrangement of the herbarium] be paid by the treasurer; and that Dr. Torrey be authorized to employ a curator at a compensation of $20 per month, and that payment at that rate be made from the first day of May last.

DR. TORREY'S DWELLING.

1860, Dec. 3. The standing committee was authorized to put in order the house intended for Dr. Torrey.

1868, April 6. *Resolved*, That it be permitted to Dr. Torrey, on condition that his services to the institution be continued, to reside in the house on the college ground now occupied by him, for two years from and after the first of May next.

HONORS.

1840, Sept. 6. *Resolved,* Unanimously, that a committee be raised, to be denominated "the committee of honors;" that it consist of five members to be appointed by ballot; and that all vacancies therein be filled in the same manner; that one member of the committee shall go out of office on the first Monday of November in each year, the order of retirement to be determined by lot at the first meeting of the committee; and that all propositions for the conferring of honorary degrees be referred to this committee, to consider and report upon; and that no such degree shall be conferred unless the proposition shall have been reported upon by it, unless by the unanimous consent of the board.

1853, April 4. *Resolved,* That, hereafter, in the conferring of honorary degrees, the board will act upon the cases reported upon by the committee of honors, individually and by ballot; and that no honorary degree shall be conferred unless the candidate shall have received the votes of the major part of the trustees present at the meeting.

INQUIRY INTO THE STATE OF THE COLLEGE, COMMITTEE ON.

1855, Oct. 2. *Resolved,* That a select committee of five be elected by ballot,

1. To inquire into the propriety of amending the statutes so as to allow a discretion to the president to grant vacations or intermissions of public lectures besides those prescribed by the statutes; and under what circumstances, if any, such discretion ought to be allowed.

2. To consult and take the statements of the president and other members of the faculty, and librarian, and any other persons, to be expressed in oral answers to such questions as the committee may think proper to propound, relating to the subjects of inquiry directed by this resolution; and that the questions and answers be reduced to writing and reported by the committee.

3. That the committee inquire by such means and otherwise as they may deem necessary, into the past and present administration of the system of education and discipline of the college and grammar school, and into the condition of both such branches of the institution, as respects government, order, discipline, and efficient and thorough instruction, and as respects the observance of the statutes.

4. That the committee report fully upon the matters referred, stating their opinion thereon; and if they shall find any defects either in the statutes or in their practical application, that they state the causes of the same, and recommend such measures as they may deem necessary for their correction; suggesting such alterations as in their judgment will tend to the orderly government of the students, and to the ascertaining and enforcing their attention and proficiency.

Messrs. Ogden, Betts, Bradford, Allen, and Anderson were appointed the committee.

1856, July 7. After a preamble setting forth the facts connected with the appointment of two committees of the board, the one on a proposed course of university instruction, and the other on the present condition of the college and grammar school, and the instructions heretofore given to those committees, two resolutions were presented and passed, of which the second, referring to this committee, was as follows:

Resolved, That the inquiries of the committee of inquiry extend to the taking of the statements and opinions of the president and other members of the faculty, and any other persons, as to the principles and details of a plan of university education proper to be adopted in connection with the under-graduate course of this institution, in order that the evidence, statements, and opinions obtained on this and the subjects of the course of instruction in the college and grammar school may be submitted to the committee on the course, for their action and report.

1856, July 7. A communication from professor M'Culloh suggesting certain alterations in his department, was referred to the committee of inquiry in the state of the college, with power.

The committee resolved, in accordance with the request of professor M'Culloh, that a working laboratory be fitted up under the direction of the professor of natural philosophy and chemistry in the rooms now allotted to him, in so far as may be necessary to test the advantages of instructing the students of the college in chemistry with the aid of experiments and manipulations performed by themselves, under the direction and superintendence of the professor, and that the sum of two hundred dollars, suggested by the professor, be appropriated for that purpose, and for furnishing the necessary glassware, materials, and attendance, to be expended under his direction. This action having been reported to the board on the 6th Oct., 1856, it was

1856, Oct. 6. *Resolved*, That the clerk furnish to the president a copy of the resolution respecting a working laboratory, adopted by the committee of inquiry and reported by them to this board, and that the president communicate all such resolutions to the board of the college.

1856, Dec. 1. *Resolved*, That the committee of inquiry be authorized to have one hundred and fifty copies of their proceedings printed.

Rev. Dr. Haight was added to the committee of inquiry.

INQUIRY INTO THE STATE OF THE COLLEGE. 47

1857, Feb. 2. *Resolved,* That the committee of inquiry be, and hereby are, authorized to incur such expenses as may in their judgment be necessary in the prosecution of their inquiries; and the treasurer is requested to pay all bills for the future or past expenses of such committee, which shall be approved by them.

Resolved, That the system of volunteering lately introduced by the professor of mathematics into his department, be referred to the committee of inquiry, and report respecting the same with all convenient speed.

1857, April 6. *Resolved,* That the select committee of inquiry extend their inquiry to those proceedings in the college which appear in the minutes of the faculty of their proceedings since the last stated meeting of the board, and report with as little delay as possible upon the causes of defective discipline in the college.

1857, April 20. The committee of inquiry were requested to furnish the members of the board with such parts of the testimony taken before them as may have been printed, for the private use of the members.

1858, Nov. 1. Authority was given to the committee of inquiry to print their forthcoming report.

1858, Dec. 6. The report of the committee of inquiry was presented by Mr. Ogden and was accepted; whereupon it was

Resolved, That the printed copies of the evidence and of the report be deposited in the college library, and that forty copies be bound.

INSTRUCTION, COURSE OF, AND COMMITTEE ON THE COURSE.

1853, Oct. 3. *Resolved,* That it be referred to a committee of three, to be elected by ballot, to inquire whether it is expedient to take any, and what measures, for the removal of the seat of the college ; and in the event of such removal, whether any, and what changes ought to be made in the under-graduate course; and whether it would be expedient to establish a system of university education in addition to such under-graduate course, either in continuation thereof or otherwise. That such committee report fully as to the principles and details of any plan that they may recommend, and whether in their opinion it can be successfully carried into execution ; and in connection therewith that they consider whether, for the more effectual carrying out of such plan, and extending the benefits of this institution, it ought to afford rooms and commons, or rooms alone, for resident students, and ought to have its seat isolated.

Mr. Betts, Dr. Anderson, and governor Fish, were named as the committee, to which, December 19, was added Dr. Knox.

1853, Nov. 7. On the 7th of November, this committee reported at some length, presenting resolutions which were made the special order for Monday, November 14th, and which were then considered, and after amendment passed as follows :

1853, Nov. 14. *Resolved,* That it is expedient that the college should be removed from its present locality with all reasonable diligence.

Resolved, That a committee of three be appointed to inquire whether suitable accommodations can be procured in the upper part of the city for a chapel and lecture rooms, and for the library and apparatus ; so that the removal of the college, if deemed expedient, may take place at an early period in the ensuing spring or summer.

INSTRUCTION, COMMITTEE ON COURSE OF.

1854, March 6.   The following resolutions of the board seem to have been suggested by the committee on the course:

Resolved, That in view of the approaching necessity of dividing and redistributing the duties of the existing chairs, including the one now vacant, the subjects entrusted to those chairs, their titles, hours of attendance, and modes of compensation be considered as necessarily held *ad interim,* and liable to modifications, to take effect at no distant day.

Resolved, That in furtherance of the proposed modifications, the professors be invited to present to the committee on the course such improvements on the college plan of education as they, in the exercise of their discretion, may deem it proper to suggest; and that the committee be authorized to address to the professors such questions in relation to the college course as it may be thought advisable to propose.

Resolved, That a copy of these resolutions be sent to each professor.

1854, May 1.   The committee on the course reported progress, and asked an appropriation to enable them to print.

1854, July 24.   The committee on the course made an elaborate report, embodying suggestions as to the form of a statute to regulate the course of instruction in the college in all branches of education. Whereupon it was resolved that the report be printed, and that the suggestions for a statute be likewise printed.

1854, Oct. 14.   The committee on the course were authorized, by resolution of the board, to prepare a statute defining the proposed course, and to report the same to the board.

1854, Nov. 6.   The following resolutions were submitted by the committee on the college course for the consideration of the trustees:

Resolved, That until the augmentation of the college revenue shall admit of the actual commencement of the co-ordinate course of study recommended by the committee on the course, the present course be continued, with such modifications, from time to time, as circumstances may require; and that the building or buildings contemplated on the college property, between Forty-seventh and Fifty-first streets, be erected in reference to the accommodations demanded for the successful prosecution of the course now proposed.

Resolved, That as soon as the augmented college income shall permit, a suitable building or buildings be erected on the above property or elsewhere, adapted to the scheme of co-ordinate instruction recommended by the committee on the course.

Resolved, That, for the purpose of carrying out the plan of extended instruction, this board look to the creation of as many additional professorships as are necessary to conduct the co-ordinate course, including therein such parts of the three faculty courses as may be appropriately assigned to the co-ordinate professors; the remaining duties of the three faculty courses to be discharged by a third order of professors, who shall commence their labors with the senior year.

It was ordered that these resolutions be printed, and sent to each trustee.

1854, Nov. 23. The following resolutions were offered by Mr. Ruggles, to be considered at a future meeting:

Resolved, That the interests of the college require, in revising its course of study, the due recognition and intermixture of moral, mental, and physical science with thorough classical training, as elements equally essential in its intellectual culture, and that they be pursued in a single course to the end of the third or junior year.

Resolved, That in view of its greatly enlarged resources, the college ought now to establish supplemental courses in continuation of the studies of the first three years, without reference to professional or artistic pursuits, but solely for higher culture in learning and science, to extend for three additional years, with degrees, as at present, at the end of the first or senior year, and with an unrestricted choice of studies during the two succeeding years.

Resolved, That the college, as soon as its means will permit, may advantageously establish special and separate professional and artistic schools, in connection with the liberal arts and sciences, to be taught in its general course.

Resolved, That the trustees fully concur in that portion of the report of the committee on the college course which regards as fundamental, "the habitual recognition, on a positive christian basis, of an authority above all human will," and that in enlarging their plan of instruction, full and special provision should be made for teaching the connection and mutual support of revelation and the various branches of human science and learning.

Resolved, That in erecting college buildings on the lands between Forty-seventh and Fifty-first streets, a portion should be constructed with special reference to the thorough teaching of the various departments of physical science and natural history, with the necessary apparatus and scientific collections; that such portion should be so built as to admit of enlargement from time to time, with the progress of collections, and that it should be commenced and completed at the same time as the other portions of the building, and be made fire-proof.

On subsequent motion,

Resolved, That these resolutions be printed, and sent to every trustee.

1854, Dec. 4. *Resolved*, That the consideration of the resolutions introduced on the 6th November, 1854, by the committee on the course, and those on the 23d of the same month, be postponed until the committee on the course shall report a statute.

52 INSTRUCTION, COMMITTEE ON COURSE OF.

1855, June 5.   The committee on the course reported that they were ready to present the statute required of them, whenever the board should be pleased to receive it.

1856, July 7.   *Resolved,* That the committee on the course of instruction consider the course of instruction proper to be pursued in the grammar school, taken as a part of the system of education to be adopted by the institution, and report upon the same with the same particularity as upon other branches of the subject committed to them.

1857, Feb. 2.   On motion of Mr. Ruggles, it was

Resolved, That the following resolutions, and also the resolutions offered by him on the 23d November, 1854, be referred to the committee on the course :

Resolved, That a professorship of geology, a professorship of natural history and physiology, a professorship of physical and commercial geography, and a professorship of American history be, and the same are hereby established in the college.

Resolved, That every professor in the college, of any department of physical or natural science, annually present to the trustees a report or memoir on its advancement during the year.

Resolved, That five thousand dollars be expended annually in maintaining prize scholarships in the post-graduate course.

1857, April 20.   *Resolved,* That it be referred to the committee of the whole in charge of the proposed statute, to consider the several resolutions of this board, under which the departments of mathematics and of ethics have been divided, and new professorships established in those departments, and to inquire,

Whether an assistant professor or tutor in the department of mathematics will not better subserve the interests of the college than a separate professorship of astronomy. Also,

Whether the department of ethics may not be more advantageously divided into two instead of three separate chairs, and that the committee report at a future meeting of this board; and in case any alteration of the plan heretofore adopted for the division of the said department be deemed advisable, they may report resolutions to carry the same into effect, and assigning the proper titles to the several professorships which they may propose.

1857, March 2. The statute so long delayed was presented by the committee on the course, prefaced by a report of some length. It proposed a course of study substantially similar to the course previously pursued in college up to the end of the junior year; but provided for the creation, in the senior year, of three departments, viz.: letters, science, and jurisprudence, the subjects to be taught very much by lecture.

It provided further, that from the commencement of the sophomore year, there should be a co-ordinate course, embracing a larger amount of scientific, and a less amount of classical, study than the other. The degree of bachelor of arts to be conferred on those who should pursue the regular course to the satisfaction of the trustees and faculty, for four years; and the degree of bachelor of science to be conferred on those who should similarly pursue the full course of study in that course.

It provided also for professorships in modern languages, additional to the Gebhard professorship, viz.: in spanish, italian, and french.

In the post-graduate department, it provided for the creation of a school of letters, a school of science, and a school of jurisprudence. The school of letters to embrace moral and mental philosophy, including an analysis of the moral and intellectual powers; æsthetics, or the principles of taste and art; the history of philosophy; appropriate literature of the greeks and romans; oriental and modern languages, as far as possible; comparative philology. The school of science to embrace mechanics and physics; astronomy; chemistry and mineralogy; geology and palæontology; engineering, mining and metallurgy; arts of design; history of science; natural history. And the school of jurisprudence to embrace modern history; political economy; the principles of natural and international law; civil and common law, as far as possible; the writings of the greeks and romans appropriate to these last subjects.

The report and draft of statute were ordered to be printed.

1857, May 11. The statute reported by the committee on the course of university instruction was considered in committee of the whole, amended and reported complete. After which it was ordered to be printed for the use of the board.

1857, June 15. Mr. Peter Cooper, having signified to the president his desire that the building recently erected by him for the "union of science and art," should be used by this college for its university course, in whole or in part, a committee of five, consisting of president King, Dr. Beadle, Mr. Van Wagenen, Mr. Bradford, and Mr. Allen, was appointed to confer with Mr. Cooper on the subject.

No report from this committee appears upon the minutes.

Resolved, That the president be directed to prepare, on consultation with the faculty, and to report to this board for their action, as soon as possible, appropriate courses of college study and corresponding tables of attendance, to go into effect at the commencement of the ensuing college year, with the understanding—

1. That there shall be an authoritative course of study to the end of the junior year, and in the following year three courses of elective study, one of letters, one of science, and one of jurisprudence.

2. That the students of the single course be engaged with their instructors twenty hours a week, and that a student of a senior course be enabled to attend at least fifteen hours a week in the department in which he may matriculate.

3. That until university classes be duly organized and ready to attend, the professors engaged at full salaries meet the college classes, or sections of them, for purposes of instruction, at least five hours a week, or as nearly so as mutual accommodation will permit.

Resolved, further, That the president, on such consultation, be likewise requested to prepare a table of studies to be pursued in the post-graduate or university course, commencing at the opening of the term in September next, and to report such table to the trustees on or before the first Monday of July next:

In the school of letters—

1. Lectures by the professor of religion, natural and revealed.

2. Lectures by the professor of history.

3. Lectures by the professor of literature.

4. Lectures by the professor of greek.

5. Lectures by the professor of latin.

6. Lectures by the professor of german.

In the school of science—

1. Lectures by the professor of physics.

2. Lectures by the professor of chemistry.

3. Lectures by the professor of astronomy.

4. Lectures by the professor of mathematics.

1857, July 6. The president made a report on the matters committed to him on the 15th June. On the same day the statute reported May 11, regulating the course of study for all the four years, and expressly prescribing the subjects to be taught in the several departments of letters, science, and jurisprudence during the senior year, was adopted. The same statute further provided for a university course, to embrace three schools, viz., a school of letters, a school of science, and a school of jurisprudence, and set forth the subjects to be taught in the same. These schools were to be open to any persons; and any one pursuing, for the space of two years, such of the studies of the same as the trustees should prescribe, to the satisfaction of the faculty and trustees, was to receive the degree of master of arts. The statute provided further for the establishment of fellowships, with or without stipends, and for prize scholarships.

1857, Sept. 17. The president reported two schemes of attendance under the new statute, the consideration of which was made the special order for a special meeting to be held on 1857, Sept. 23. the 23d. On that day the scheme for the three lower classes was amended and adopted; and the scheme for the senior year was referred to a select committee consisting of Dr. Haight, Dr. Spring, and Mr. Ogden.

1857, Sept. 17. A committee was appointed to consider the propriety of introducing into the scheme of instruction, a course of instruction in architecture. No report from this committee appears on the minutes.

1857, Oct. 5. The scheme of instruction was reported complete, and adopted by the board.

A scheme of attendance, in accordance with the new statute on the course of instruction, having been reported by the committee, and adopted with amendments suggested by the faculty, a resolution was adopted, assigning to the several officers of the faculty the subjects which they would be required to teach.

A committee was appointed to inquire into the expediency of establishing a chair of design and drawing. This committee made a report at the following meeting, which was laid on the table and never afterward called up.

1857, Nov. 9. *Resolved*, That it be referred to the president and the Gebhard professor, with power, to devise a scheme of instruction in the german language and literature, with an understanding that the study shall be voluntary.

Resolved, That it be referred to the president and faculty to devise and report a scheme of attendance and instruction in the other modern languages and in drawing.

1857, Dec. 7.   The report on instruction in german, required by resolution of November 9, was made by the president, whereupon the following resolution was adopted:

Resolved, That in conformity with the scheme reported in relation to instruction in the german language, &c., two prizes for the german—one of thirty dollars, the other of twenty dollars—be awarded annually to the best student in each of the classes into which it is proposed to divide the students; provided that in every case the award be made to those among the competitors in each class sustaining the best examination, the decision to rest with the professor of the department and the president.

1858, Feb. 1.   Reports from the president and faculty, required by resolution of November 9, on drawing and the other modern languages besides german, were presented and referred to the committee on the course. February 1, 1858, the committee on the course reported, and a resolution was passed directing that, when it should be deemed by the trustees expedient to establish classes in french and spanish, there should be formed two classes, which should receive two hours of instruction per week each; the students to proceed from the lower to the higher class on examination, and the course of instruction to be left to the direction of the several professors, subject to the direction of the trustees.

It was further resolved that the organization of a department of free-hand drawing should be considered in connection with an university course, when the report expected on that subject from the president and faculty should be made: and further, that the instruction in industrial drawing should be committed to the charge of the adjunct professor of mathematics.

A resolution was passed requesting the president to present to the board a report on university instruction, " in conformity with the request heretofore made." [The request referred to must be that embraced in the resolutions of June 15, 1857, since no other appears in the minutes. It would seem, however, by the minutes of July 6, quoted above, that the report called for had been made already.]

1858, March 1. The president reported two schemes of university instruction ; and the board resolved to meet on the following Monday, for their consideration.

1858, March 8. The special object of this adjourned meeting being under consideration, Mr. Ruggles presented a paper containing several subjects of inquiry touching the same, which, along with the reports of the president, were referred to a select committee, consisting of Bishop Potter, Mr. Betts, Mr. Ruggles, Mr. Van Wagenen, and Mr. Allen.

1858, April 5. The select committee appointed March 8, made a report proposing to initiate the organization, at the opening of the fall term, of the several schools established by statute, by giving instruction in the several schools as follows :

SCHOOL OF LETTERS.

Ethics, history in connection with the school of jurisprudence, greek, latin, history of philosophy, english language and literature.

SCHOOL OF SCIENCE.

Mechanics and physics, astronomy, chemistry, geology and natural history, mathematics, including engineering and physical geography.

SCHOOL OF JURISPRUDENCE.

Political philosophy, history in connection with the school of letters, natural and international law, constitutional law, municipal law, moot courts, appropriate greek and latin literature.

The committee advise that instruction in the schools of letters and jurisprudence should be given in some central and easily accessible place, and in that of science in the college, where are the laboratory, cabinets, apparatus, and collections.

Also, that fees in these schools should be paid by graduates of the college as well as by others—the fees paid by graduates to be at the disposal of the trustees, and those paid by others to go to the professors.

They further recommend that the terms of instruction in the university course shall extend from the first of October to the first of June, with the usual intermissions. And in regard to the tenure of office, they suggest that no positive rule be laid down for the present, but that appointments be more or less permanent, as may from time to time be determined by the board of trustees.

Whereupon the following resolution was adopted:

Resolved, That the recommendations of the committee be approved, except that the subject of fees be reserved for further consideration by this board; and that it be referred to the same committee to provide necessary accommodations for instruction, as proposed, in some central situation; and to take such other measures as they may deem expedient for organizing and carrying on the proposed course; and that they report as soon as practicable whether any and what additional instructors will be required, to the end that this board may take measures for their selection.

On motion of Mr. Ruggles, it was further resolved to add the "science and art of education" to the subjects to be taught in the school of letters.

1858, May 17. Mr. Bradford was added to the committee.

1858, June 21. The select committee on the university course reported the following resolutions, which were adopted *seriatim*, viz.:

Resolved,—First, That the post-graduate instruction of the college commence annually on the first Monday of November, and close on the first Saturday of June following.

Second, That the committee on post-graduate instruction be authorized to secure the services, for such portions of the next two years as they may be able, of professor James D. Dana in the department of geology and natural history; of professor Arnold Guyot, in physical geography and kindred subjects; of Mr. George P. Marsh, in the English language; at a compensation to each not exceeding fifteen hundred dollars annually; and of professor Theodore W. Dwight, or such other competent instructor as said committee may select, for the elementary branch of the law department; to be compensated by fees to be guaranteed by the college to amount to fifteen hundred dollars annually; and of any other instructors in any department of jurisprudence, science, or letters presented by the statute, who will accept fees in full compensation.

Third, That the said committee be authorized to arrange all the necessary details with the several professors of the college in respect to lectures and other instruction to be given by them in the post-graduate course; but all such arrangements shall expire with the close of the next collegiate year.

Fourth, That the several professors and instructors in the post-graduate course shall make such examinations at least once in every fortnight, as may enable them to determine the relative proficiency of students competing for university degrees or honors.

Fifth, That the post-graduate instruction in mathematics, physics, astronomy, and chemistry, be conducted at the college buildings, and in the other branches at the building of the historical society, or such other locality as the committee may find necessary.

Sixth, That a sum not exceeding fifteen hundred dollars be expended under the direction of the committee, for such diagrams, drawings, and specimens as may be necessary in the courses of geology, natural history, and physical geography; and if the professor of chemistry so elect, the sum of five hundred dollars heretofore appropriated for a chemical cabinet may be expended in apparatus and materials needed in the post-graduate course.

Seventh, That fees not exceeding five dollars for each course of general lectures in the post-graduate course shall be received by the college, to be hereafter appropriated as the trustees may direct; which rate, in the discretion of the committee, may be reduced to three dollars for graduates of not more than three years' standing of the college, of the university of the city of New York, and of the free academy.

Eighth, That fees for special or technical instruction, to be approved by said committee, may be received by the several professors or instructors giving such instruction in the post-graduate course.

It was further ordered that the president be authorized to give public notice, at the approaching commencement, of the adoption by the college of a scheme of post-graduate studies, and that the same is to go into operation during the next ensuing term.

1858, Dec. 6. Bishop Potter was excused from serving on the committee on post-graduate instruction.

1859, April 4. The following resolution would seem to have been adopted at the instance of the committee on the course, or for the benefit of the committee, but this does not appear from the minutes:

Resolved, That it be referred to the board of the college, and they are requested to frame and report to this board a scheme of instruction for the under-graduate course, in which shall be specified both the subjects and

extent of instruction in each department * * * * *
These may be definitely prescribed, and may be so limited that the combination of the courses in all the departments may form a general course which shall be perfectly within the ability of the students thoroughly to master in each and all its parts; and also to frame a scheme of attendance in conformity with the scheme of instruction. In the departments of the greek and latin classics the board is requested to devise alternative courses for each session, etc., etc.

Nothing appears on the minutes of the board indicating that the report here called for was ever made, but, on the 4th of February, 1861, a special committee of the board previously appointed to prepare a plan for instruction in astronomy reported that " the consideration of this matter is necessarily connected with an examination of the entire scheme prepared by the faculty."

Whereupon the following resolution was passed. The scheme referred to may possibly be that which was called for in the resolution of April 4, 1859:

1861, Feb. 4. *Resolved,* That the report of the faculty on the proposed course of study be printed under the direction of the president, and that he direct copies to be sent to each of the trustees before the next meeting of the board.

1861, Feb. 25. At a subsequent meeting of the board the following action was taken relating to the same report:

Resolved, That the report of the board of the college upon the course of study be referred to a committee of three members of this board, to consider the recommendations of such report, etc., etc.

Mr. Allen, Mr. Strong, and Mr. Rutherfurd were appointed the committee.

No report of the committee appears in the minutes of the board.

INSTRUCTION, COMMITTEE ON COURSE OF. 63

1859, May 2. *Resolved*, That the president report to the board at their next stated meeting the particulars of the result of the course of university instruction given during the last winter; and that the treasurer report the amount of expense attending such course.

No report from the president in response to this resolution appears on the minutes. The treasurer, however, reported, June 6, the particulars of expenditure actually incurred on account of the university course for the year, or still remaining due, as follows: compensation to lecturers, $3,000; drawings and illustrations, $458.10; printing and advertising, $485.18; rent of Historical society's rooms, $600—total $4,543.28.

1859, June 6. *Resolved*, That the committee on post-graduate instruction report to this board at its next meeting on the expediency of establishing a practical school of science; and, if they deem it expedient, to report such measures as are necessary for carrying the same into execution, and the plan and probable expense thereof.

1859, Oct. 3. It was resolved that any professors belonging to the college faculty, who might deliver lectures in any of the post-graduate courses, should be allowed to receive the fees paid for such lectures, provided they should pay the expenses of advertisement, and should give notice to the president of their desire to receive such fees; and provided further that this resolution should not apply to receiving fees from students in the law school.

1861, June 3. *Resolved*, That the division of the senior class into three schools be abolished at the end of the present academic year, and that the course of study thereafter be the same for the whole class.

1861, June 21. The select committee on the post-graduate course were discharged at their own request.

[This was the committee appointed March 8, 1858. The committee on the general course of instruction continued still in existence.]

1863, Oct. 5.	Rev. Dr. Dix was appointed to the committee on the course in place of Mr. Allen, deceased.
1863, Oct. 15.	*Resolved*, That the entire subject of instruction in the college and its distribution among the various departments, be referred to the committee on the course, together with bishop Potter and judge Bradford; also the subject of the professorship of physics and the expediency of abolishing it and distributing its branches among the other departments, with directions to report thereon with all convenient speed.

The following resolutions were adopted on the recommendation of the committee on the course:

1863, Dec. 7. *Resolved*, That on the termination of the present academic year, analytical geometry and the calculus be removed to the senior year, and their study be made optional.

Resolved, That after the current year, the hours allotted to the mathematical department for the instruction of the junior class be reduced from five to three, and that one hour additional be given to the greek and latin departments each.

Resolved, That the department of physics be continued as now established, and that the chair be filled as soon as may be conveniently done.

Resolved, That the subjects of instruction in the department of physics be taught without reference to the calculus, and in a more popular and intelligible manner, the professor using, so far as practicable, text-books.

Resolved, That a course of the history of modern literature be introduced into professor Nairne's department, together with the history of moral and intellectual philosophy, and that the study of pure metaphysics be reduced.

Resolved, That it be referred to the special committee to make and report to the board, a scheme of study and attendance, based on the preceding resolutions, as well for the permanent course as for the remainder of the current year.

1865, Feb. 6.

Resolved, That ancient geography be, after the present academic year, excluded from the course of study in college; and that, after the next academic year, it be placed among the requisites for admission to the freshman class.

Professor Ordronaux, having presented to the board a proposition to deliver a voluntary course of lectures on anatomy and physiology to the members of the senior class of under-graduates, and requested that hours might be assigned for the purpose, it was

Resolved, That while this board fully appreciates the value of the instruction which it is proposed by the professor of medical jurisprudence in the school of law to give to the under-graduates in the college, it does not appear to be practicable at the present time to make the arrangements which would be necessary to ensure the success of the course of lectures proposed.

Resolved, That it be referred to the president to report a proper text-book in ancient geography, and the extent of instruction to be required for entrance.

1865, July 6.

Resolved, That until further order of this board, instruction in history and political economy be given by the professor of philosophy and english literature, under the direction of the president.

1865, Oct. 9.

Resolved, That the subject of mechanics, embracing the general doctrines of statics and dynamics, with their applications to solids, fluids, and gases, be transferred to the professor of mathematics and astronomy, and hereafter, until the further order of this board, be taught by him.

INVENTORY OF MOVABLE PROPERTY.

1838, Dec. 1. *Resolved*, That all officers having charge of movable property of the college, prepare duplicate inventories of the same, one copy to be left with the president, and one with the clerk for the use of this board.

1862, April 7. *Resolved*, That the president be requested to obtain from the several professors a catalogue of the apparatus under their charge, belonging to the college, specifying as far as possible the date of purchase, and the price paid for each piece.

1862, June 2. The committee to whom were referred the reports of the professors upon the apparatus belonging to the college, recommend, June 2d, 1862, that the original reports when signed by the professors severally making them, be filed with the clerk of the board; and that copies of the same be kept in a book prepared for that purpose, and be kept at the college by the president. The report was accepted and the recommendations contained were adopted.

LAW SCHOOL.

1858, May 17. The committee on university instruction made a report recommending the organization of a school of law. Whereupon, on motion, it was

Resolved, That a law school be established on the basis recommended by the committee, such school to go into operation in the ensuing autumn.

The committee on university instruction presented the following resolutions which were adopted:

1859, May 2. *Resolved*, That there be added to the corps of instructors in the law school, such gratuitous lecturers upon common and civil law, and equity jurisprudence, as shall be determined upon by the consulting committee hereafter created. Also, that courses of lectures be established upon medical jurisprudence, upon political philosophy, including a history of government and of political literature, and upon ethics. The two latter courses to be delivered by professors attached to the under-graduate course of instruction, and the time of the delivery of the lectures to be determined by the professors and lecturers.

A committee, consisting of the legal members of the present committee, with Messrs. Ogden, Strong, and Fish, and the professors in the law school, was authorized to choose the lecturers named in this resolution.

PRIZES.

Resolved, That there be established a series of prizes in the law school to consist of the following sums:

A first prize of $250, for excellence of attainment in legal science, &c.
A second prize of $200.
A third prize of $150.
A fourth prize of $100.

The particular details in relation to the above prizes, and likewise the scheme of instruction and attendance, shall be determined by the committee and the professor of municipal law.

LIBRARY.

1859, Dec. 5. *Resolved,* That the chairman of the board of trustees, the president of the college, the treasurer, the clerk, and the professor of municipal law, shall be the law library committee, and shall make such rules, and such recommendations to the trustees as they shall deem expedient, and also shall direct the expenditures for the purchase of books. The professor of municipal law shall

1860, Jan. 9.

1861, June 24.

be the secretary of such committee, and may call meetings of the same.

Resolved, That an appropriation be made from the funds of the college for the purchase of books for the law library, under the direction of the law library committee, to the amount of three hundred dollars per annum, commencing with the collegiate year 1859—this amount to be payable on the draft of the professor at the beginning of each year.

This appropriation was, however, reduced to one hundred and fifty dollars in 1861, and it was further ordered that the professor of municipal law be limited to an expenditure of not over three hundred dollars for printing and advertising of whatever kind, done under his direction for the law school.

REGULATIONS CONCERNING EXAMINATIONS AND PRIZES.

1860, Feb. 6.

The committee on the law school reported the following rules and regulations, in relation to examinations and prizes, which were adopted:

1. EXAMINATIONS.

There shall be one oral examination of candidates for the degree of bachelor of laws, at the close of the second year. The examination is to be conducted by the professors in the law school, and is distinct from that hereinafter established for prizes.

2. DEGREES.

The degree of bachelor of laws shall be conferred upon such students as shall pass an examination satisfactory to the professor of municipal law.

3. PRIZES.

The rules respecting the adjudication of prizes are as follows:

First—There shall be an examination of the candidates for prizes at the close of each collegiate year. The first examination will occur in May, 1860. All members of the present senior class shall be entitled to compete for the prizes. After this year candidates must be connected with the law school for two collegiate years.

Second—The test of excellence shall be two-fold :

a. By an examination in writing in answer to printed questions.

b. By essays prepared upon such legal topics as may be suggested. The prizes shall be adjudicated upon the combined excellence of the essays and examination. Diligence and regularity of attendance upon the prescribed exercises of the school shall form an element in reaching the conclusion.

Third—The following directions must be observed by candidates in preparing essays :

a. The essays shall be written upon white letter-paper of the best quality, with a margin of an inch wide. Only two pages of each sheet should be written on. The chirography should be fair and legible. The essay should not exceed ten sheets in length, or three-fourths of an hour in delivery, if spoken.

b. The positions taken in the essays, if debatable, should be fortified by the citation of authorities. Where the point is reasonably well settled, a single decisive and leading authority shall suffice. In other cases more are admissible.

c. Conciseness and clearness of expression, accuracy of statement and close reasoning should be carefully studied by the essayists.

d. The essays should be signed with a fictitious name, and be accompanied by a sealed envelope, upon the outside of which shall be written the fictitious name attached to the essay, and within a slip of paper containing the real name of the author. The essays should be delivered to the professor of municipal law, on or before May 15, 1860.

e. The unsuccessful essays shall be returned to the authors with the envelopes unopened. The successful shall belong to the college and shall be preserved in bound volumes for the use of the law library.

f. Any essays which have received honorable mention from the committee of award, and have failed to receive a prize, may, with the consent of the authors, be bound with the prize essays.

Fourth—The examinations upon the printed questions shall be made as follows:

a. Those who intend to compete for the prizes shall enter their names in a book provided for that purpose before May 1. If among those names there are any who have been wanting in a reasonable degree in punctuality they shall be informed, before examination, that they may fail of obtaining the prize.

b. The professor of municipal law shall call a session of the candidates at such time, near the close of the collegiate year, as may be convenient. He shall furnish at the opening of the session, the printed papers to the students, who shall write their answers in their presence upon paper similar to that provided for the essays, with a similar margin. During this session there shall be a general silence observed, except such necessary questions as may be addressed to the professor, and there shall be expressly no communication of the candidates with each other regarding answers. A failure to observe these rules will work a forfeiture of the right to receive a prize.

c. After this session is finished, the answers to the printed questions shall be signed with the fictitious names attached to the essays, and enclosed in an envelope, as before. The answers shall belong to the college.

Fifth—The essays and answers shall thereupon be transmitted to a committee on prizes, consisting of three members of the legal profession, who are to be selected by the law committee of the college. The report of this committee will be communicated to the clerk of the college in writing.

Sixth—The names of the successful condidates and the substance of the report shall be published in the principal daily papers in the city at the expense of the college. Notice will also be given by letter to the successful candidates.

Seventh—The prizes shall be awarded at the option of the recipient, in money, medals or books; when no notice is given to the contrary the award will be in money until otherwise ordered. The professor of municipal law will countersign all drafts upon the treasurer before they can become available.

Resolved, That it shall be the duty of the professor of municipal law and other professors of law in the law school, with the law committee of this board, on the expiration of the course of study of the senior class in each year, to examine the members of that class and thereby to ascertain their fitness to receive the degree of bachelor of laws, and to be admitted to practice in the courts of this state, in pursuance of the law passed April 7, 1860. After each examination shall be concluded, the said professor or professors and the said committee, or any three of them, being counsellors at law, shall recommend in writing to this board, such of the said students as they may deem properly qualified to receive the said degree and to be admitted, and thereupon, on the approval of such recommendation, a diploma in the form reported to the trustees and approved, will be granted to each student so recommended; which shall be signed by the president and such members of the board of examiners as shall attend the examination; and the seal of the college shall be affixed thereunto.

1860, May 21. *Resolved,* That the clerk be authorized to affix the seal of the college to all certificates of prizes and to all diplomas which may be issued in the law school.

LAW SCHOOL.

1861, May 20. *Resolved,* That the existing system of prizes be modified so that the second prize of two hundred dollars be awarded for excellence in the department of political science, and that the students competing for other prizes be not required to attend in any department except that of municipal law.

LAW FACULTY.

1861, June 3. *Resolved,* That the law committee be instructed to consider the propriety of the establishment of a law faculty, in order that the same may be established by the beginning of the next academic year.

LAW SCHOOL.—REGULATIONS FOR SUPPORT OF.

1864, Feb. 1. 1. The tuition fees shall be one hundred dollars for each year for all students who shall hereafter enter the school, and for those who are now students, seventy-five dollars.

2. The professor of municipal law and the treasurer may, in special cases, remit the fee in whole or in part.

3. The fees shall be collected by the professor of municipal law, and be from time to time as received, paid by him to the treasurer.

4. The rent, and the necessary repairs of the building occupied by the school, and an annual expenditure of two hundred and fifty dollars for the library, shall be paid by the college out of its general fund.

5. The amount received for fees shall each year be applied, *first* to the payment of all expenses of the school except those which are to be paid, as before mentioned, out of the general fund of the college ; *second,* to the payment of the professor of municipal law, six thousand dollars, so far as the receipts for the year may be sufficient for that purpose. Of the balance remaining, after such application, one-half shall be paid to the professor of municipal law, and one-half shall be retained by the college.

6. The said salary of the professor of municipal law shall be paid in each year three thousand dollars on the first day of November, and the remainder at the end of the academic year of the school, so far as the receipts of the year shall suffice.

7. The professor of municipal law shall be, *ex-officio*, a member of the law committee of the trustees.

8. The trustees of the college shall in all cases, on the recommendation of the law committee, decide as to the expediency of expenditures; but they will not, without the consent of the professor of municipal law, and to the diminution of his salary, employ any additional professor or assistant instructors, except in the department of municipal law.

INSTRUCTION—MISCELLANEOUS PROVISIONS.

1865, June 5. *Resolved,* That the law school committee be empowered in their discretion to authorize professor Ordronaux to prefix to his lectures a course on elementary anatomy and physiology, provided that the expenses of the necessary drawings and illustrations, &c., do not exceed three hundred dollars; and in that event, that the yearly salary of professor Ordronaux be raised to six hundred dollars, to commence on the first of October next; and that he be appointed professor of medical jurisprudence during the pleasure of the board.

1865, June 6. *Resolved,* That professor Lieber be transferred from the faculty of arts to the faculty of law; and that the law school committee be authorized to designate the subjects on which he shall lecture, and to assign the appropriate title to his chair and his duties, and the hours of his attendance; and that, hereafter, the students of the law school shall be required, so far as deemed expedient by the law school committee, to attend such portions of the lectures of professor Lieber and of the professor of municipal jurisprudence, as the law school committee (upon advisement with the several professors of the law school) shall deem proper; and that a rigid and satisfactory examination on the subjects treated of in such lectures (or such portion thereof as shall be deemed proper) shall be required of each candidate for the degree of bachelor of law, prior to his admission to that degree; and that a satisfactory examination upon such of the several subjects treated of by the several professors of the law school as the law school committee and the faculty of the law school shall deem to be expedient, shall be required of each candidate for the degree of master of laws, prior to his admission to that degree.

Resolved, That the law school committee be directed, as soon as conveniently may be, to report to this board their conclusions and judgment upon the several subjects which, by the preceding resolution, are committed to their authority or discretion, or submitted to their judgment either separately or together with any or all of the professors of the law school.

Resolved, That the salary of professor Lieber, in the faculty of law, be continued at the rate of four thousand dollars a year, until otherwise ordered by this board.

1865, Oct. 9. *Resolved*, That the professorship in the law school now held by Dr. Francis Lieber, be henceforth known as the professorship of constitutional history and public law; that it shall be the duty of the professor during each academic year to deliver one lecture weekly to each class; that lectures on the constitutional history of England be delivered to the junior class, and on that of the United States, to the senior class; and also a course on modern political history to the junior class, and on government to the senior class; that such lectures be delivered between $1\frac{1}{2}$ and $2\frac{1}{2}$ P. M.

LIBRARY.

1819, Sept. 6. *Resolved,* That a committee of five trustees be appointed, to be styled the library committee, whose duty it shall be to have a general charge of the college library; to report to the board, from time to time, such opportunities as may occur of procuring rare or valuable works; and to make such other communications respecting the library as they shall deem conducive to the welfare of this institution.

1835, Jan. 7. *Resolved,* That the members of the sophomore class be allowed to use the library under the same regulations which apply to the members of the two higher classes.

1838, April 2. *Resolved,* That the library committee be authorized to make such regulations as they may deem from time to time requisite and proper, respecting the use of the library, and also to dispose of duplicates of works contained therein, by sale or exchange, and that they report such regulations to this board.

Under the authority conferred by this resolution, the committee, two days later, adopted the code of regulations given below. These regulations have since been, from time to time, modified by the committee, and also occasionally by the trustees. It is only when amendments have been made by the trustees that the dates of the changes have been preserved.

Resolved, That such members of the freshman class as the president may specially designate, shall have the privilege of taking out books from the college library, subject to the regulations applicable to the other classes.

1839, April 1. By a resolution passed in April, 1839, the teachers of the grammar school and such students as the rector might recommend, were allowed to take books from the library, provided that the rector held himself responsible for the safe return thereof.

In 1844 the library committee was reconstructed under the following resolution:

1844, March 2. *Resolved*, That the chairman of the board of trustees, the president of the college, the clerk, the treasurer, and the librarian, shall constitute the library committee, which shall have the whole charge and direction in all matters concerning the library, subject to the board of trustees. Such committee shall meet statedly, at least four times a year, and also specially, whenever called together by its secretary, by order of any other member of the committee. If a majority shall not be present any two members, the librarian being one, shall be a quorum, complete to transact business at any meeting whereunto all the members shall have been duly summoned, subject to such regulations as shall have been made by a majority of the committee. The librarian shall be the secretary of the committee, and shall keep in a book, minutes of its proceedings to be laid before the trustees, and read from time to time to the board. And the librarian shall, at the end of every year, under the direction of the committee, make a report of the condition of the library, and of its increase during the year.

1851, Nov. 4. *Resolved*, That no debts be contracted for the library without the consent of the library committee.

1852, Dec. 13. *Resolved*, That the salary of the librarian be raised to three hundred dollars a year, to commence on the first of October last.

A second reorganization of the library committee was made in 1862, by the adoption of the following resolution:

1862, Oct. 6. *Resolved*, That the library committee shall hereafter be constituted of three trustees chosen by ballot. Immediately upon their election they shall be divided by lot into three classes, so that the time of one shall expire on the first Monday in November, 1863, of another on the first Monday in November, 1864, and of the third in November, 1865. An election by ballot shall be annually held to fill the vacancy thus occurring, and the member then to be elected shall serve for three years.

Any vacancy occurring by resignation, death, or otherwise before the expiration of the term of service of some of the members, shall be filled for the remainder of the term of the member whose place shall have become vacant, by an election by ballot.

The library committee shall have the general charge and direction of all matters concerning the library, subject always to the orders and control of the board of trustees. They shall make such regulations as they shall deem from time to time requisite and proper respecting the use of the library. They shall direct the purchases of books, and shall control and direct all expenditures of the moneys appropriated for the library.

They may dispose of duplicates of works contained therein either by sale or otherwise. The library committee shall meet statedly at least four times a year, and also specially whenever called together by a written notice (of at least two days) either signed by two members of the committee to the third, or signed by the secretary upon written request of two members of the committee.

Two members of the committee shall be a quorum competent to transact business at any meeting whereunto the members shall have been duly summoned; subject, however, to such regulations as shall have been made by the committee.

The librarian shall be secretary of the committee, and shall keep in an appropriate book the minutes of the proceedings, which shall be laid before the trustees, and read from time to time to the board. He shall give to each member of the committee a written notice of at least two days of the time and place of every meeting of the committee. He shall at the end of every year prepare and submit to the committee a full report of the condition of the library, of its increase, and of any losses or changes in the condition during the year together with any suggestions he may deem proper to recommend or submit with regard to its improvement or its management, which report shall be entered at length upon the minutes of the committee and read therewith to the board of trustees.

The librarian shall observe rigidly, and shall enforce, the rules and regulations that shall be from time to time adopted by the library committee. No debt shall be contracted for the library without the authority of the library committee. Upon the election of the committee authorized and established by the foregoing resolution, the library committee heretofore existing shall cease and be discontinued, except so far as shall be necessary to close its business, and to make report thereof to the board of trustees.

All rules and regulations heretofore made by this board, and now in existence, respecting the persons entitled to the use of the library, shall be continued until otherwise ordered.

REGULATIONS FOR THE LIBRARY.

1838, April 4. Under the authority conferred by the resolution of the trustees of April 2, 1838, given above, the committee on the library established the following regulations, under date of April 4, 1838:

1. The library shall be open from the hour of noon until 3 o'clock P. M., every day [while the college is in session, except Saturday and Sunday, and holidays established by statute.]

Subsequently amended by striking out the words in brackets, and substituting, "except Sunday, while the college is in session."

[2. The persons allowed to take out books are the trustees and officers of the college, students of the senior, junior, and sophomore classes, graduates of the college, residing in the city, who contribute the sum of four dollars annually to the support of the library; and those persons who by a donation to it of fifty dollars, or of books to that amount, have heretofore, or shall hereafter, become entitled to the use of it for life.]

This rule has been rescinded, but no record is found of its abrogation. No persons are now permitted to take books from the library except such as are designated in the college statutes.

3. No person shall be allowed to take at one time more than one volume, if in folio or in quarto; or one set, not exceeding three volumes, if in octavo or of less size.

4. A folio or a quarto may be retained four weeks; an octavo three weeks; and a duodecimo, or a volume of less size, two weeks.

5. Any person who shall detain a book longer than the time, above limited, respectively, shall forfeit and pay to the librarian, for the use of the library, for every day a volume is so detained, if it be a folio or a quarto, two cents; if an octavo or volume of less size, one cent; and until such payments be made shall not be permitted to take out any other book.

6. The above restrictions as to the number of books to be taken out, and the times for which they may be kept, shall not apply to officers of the college engaged in the instruction of its students; yet they, as well as all other persons, shall be required to return whatever books they have belonging to the college, so that they may be in their places on the shelves on the third Tuesday in June of every year.

7. The librarian shall note, in a register to be kept for that purpose, the books delivered by him; the persons who receive them; the days on which they are taken and returned, together with whatever forfeitures may have been incurred.

8. Books which, as containing fine engravings, or otherwise, are of great value, shall be marked in the catalogue with an asterisk, and shall not be taken out [without the written permission of the president.]

Subsequently amended by inserting after the word "value" the words, "or which are subjects of frequent reference, as lexicons, cyclopedias, atlases, &c.," and after the word "shall," immediately following, the words "under the direction of the library committee." Also, by striking out the words included in brackets, and substituting in their place the words "of the library."

9. No person shall, without permission of the librarian, remove books from the shelves, nor take from the library any book not delivered to him for that purpose by the librarian, who shall observe the condition of every book when given out and when returned; and the person in whose possession a book shall have sustained any injury, shall repair the same, or make satisfaction therefor, before he can take out any other book. [In case any book shall not be duly returned, the person in default shall pay its value to the librarian, or if it made part of a set, the full value of such set, the remainder of which may thereupon be taken by the person so paying for the same.]

Subsequently amended by striking out the words in brackets.

10. Each candidate for the degree of A. B. shall produce to the president a certificate from the librarian that he has returned in good order every book that he has taken out; or in default thereof, has paid its value; or if it made part of a set, the full value of such set, the remainder of which may thereupon be taken by the person so paying for the same.

This rule has been rescinded, probably at the same time with rule 2. The statutes at present provide for the cases it was intended to meet.

11. All books taken out within the four weeks next preceding the third Tuesday in July, of every year, shall be

taken under an engagement to return the same previous to that day. [The librarian shall on that day annually lay before the president a written statement of the condition of the library, together with the names of those who retain books that should have been returned, or who are otherwise in default as regards the library. He shall endeavor to have, on that day, every book belonging to the library in its place.]

Subsequently amended by substituting "June" for "July," and in place of the sentence in brackets the following, viz.: " The librarian shall endeavor to have on that day every book belonging to the library in its place."

12. During the interval between the said third Tuesday in July and the ensuing commencement, no books shall be taken from the library.

This has been rescinded; but the statutes of the college provide that no books shall be taken from the library during the interval between the third Tuesday of June and the end of the summer vacation, except such as may be taken by members of the board of the college, in conformity with the regulations.

13. In the annual report on the condition of the library, the librarian shall render an account to the library committee of all moneys received by him for fines and forfeitures, annual contributions, donations, on the exchange and sale of books, or otherwise, as librarian. He shall take care that the library be at all times well aired, and guarded against moisture, and, as far as possible, from dust. He shall see that it is carefully cleaned from time to time, as may be needed. He shall permit no loud conversation or other noise within it, that may disturb those engaged in study or research. He shall make a suitable arrangement of the books upon the shelves; shall letter or number each volume in such a manner as to indicate its place; and shall maintain a correct and complete catalogue of all books belonging to the library, and therein so denote them by their respective letters and numbers that any book may readily be found.

14. A list of all donations to the library, together with the names of donors, shall be entered in a book provided for that purpose, which shall be placed on a table in the library, and remain there for inspection.

The board of trustees has several times had under consideration the subject of the library regulations; but except while the statutes were under revision, the board has rarely interfered with the action of the library committee. A select committee on the rules was created in 1861, as follows:

<small>1861, Oct. 14.</small>

Resolved, That it be referred to a special committee of three members of this board to consider the state of the library, and the rules for the regulation of the same, and to recommend any measures which they may consider expedient.

<small>1861, Dec. 2.</small>

The committee appointed under this resolution recommended the maintenance of the existing rules, with the subjoined modifications:

Rule 5 to read as follows:

5. The above restrictions, as to the number of books, and the time for which they may be kept, shall not apply to officers of the college engaged in the instruction of its students. These officers, if desirous of retaining during the vacation books held by them previously to commencement, shall be permitted, on written order signed by the president and the acting chairman of the library committee and left with the librarian, so to retain them, along with such other publications as they may require, not exceeding in all twenty volumes for the use of each officer of instruction applying for the same.

Rule 11, to be amended by inserting after the word "library," line six, the words "and a duplicate taken before the library committee;" and to be further amended in the last clause, by inserting the word "authorized," before the word "place."

Rule 13, to be amended by inserting after the word "librarian," in the fifth line, "In this annual report to the library committee, the librarian shall state fully and clearly the number, names, and disposition of the volumes lent out or otherwise to be accounted for. A duplicate of this report, with its proper data, shall be posted up conspicuously, in some suitable place on the walls of the library, and shall remain thus exhibited until replaced by a subsequent report."

This report was referred to the committee of the whole on the statutes, but the amendments were never incorporated into the regulations. In the revised statutes, the objects aimed at by the amendments proposed to rule 11 and rule 13 have been substantially provided for.

1864, Jan. 11. *Resolved*, That it be referred to the library committee, to consider whether the rules in relation to the library may not be so modified as to give greater facilities to the professors.

1864, Feb. 1. The committee reported against any modification of the rules, but submitted to the board the question of the propriety of keeping the library open an additional number of hours daily, and also on Saturdays, and from time to time during the summer vacation.

THE PRESIDENT TO BE A PERMANENT MEMBER OF THE LIBRARY COMMITTEE.

1864, Dec. 5. *Resolved*, That the president of the college be a permanent member of the library committee.

CONTROL OF EXPENDITURES.

1868, Feb. 3. *Resolved*, That hereafter all bills for expenditures made on account of the general library be submitted, before payment, to the president for his approval; provided that no bills for books or other additions to the collection be approved by the president without the certificate of the librarian, previously obtained, that the objects have been received by him.

MEDICINE, SCHOOL OF.

1858, Feb. 1.   It having been proposed to establish a school of medicine in connection with the college, a resolution was passed declaring that this board is not prepared at present to establish such a department, and therefore that it is inexpedient to entertain any proposal for that purpose.

SCHEME OF INSTRUCTION.

1859, June 6.   A communication was received from Dr. Edward Delafield, president of the college of physicians and surgeons of the city of New York, and chairman of a committee appointed by the trustees of that institution for the purpose of opening a negotiation with the trustees of Columbia college, with a view of effecting, if possible, a union of the two institutions, proposing such union with the following provisions:

1. That each college remain an independent corporation, governing itself and not responsible for the acts of the other; but acting in concert with the other when necessary.

2. That the trustees of the college of physicians and surgeons shall have the right, by amendment to their charter, to fill their own vacancies and to appoint their professors and teachers.

3. That the degree of doctor of medicine be conferred by the joint act of the two bodies, on the recommendation of the college of physicians and surgeons.

Whereupon a committee of conference was appointed, consisting of Messrs. Betts, Ruggles, Torrey, Jones, and Bradford.

1859, June 22.   The committee of conference reported that the present charter of the college of physicians and surgeons is held from the regents of the university, and that in order to form an alliance with this college, it will be necessary to obtain from the regents a new or modified charter. The committee also reported a form of charter which it had been proposed to ask from the regents, and recommended the passage of the following resolutions, which were thereupon adopted :

Resolved, Should the regents of the university confer on the trustees of the college of physicians and surgeons, without material alteration, the proposed modified charter now presented to this board, that this board will adopt the said college of physicians and surgeons as the medical school of Columbia college.

Resolved, That this board will confer the degree of doctor of medicine on such of the graduates of the said medical school or college of physicians and surgeons [as shall be recommended to them for such degree by the trustees of said college] ;* and that the diplomas shall be publicly conferred by the president of the medical college sitting with the president of this college ; and shall be signed by the presidents of the respective colleges, and such other of the faculty as may be designated by by-laws or resolutions.

Resolved, That this board will take all necessary measures in conference with the trustees of the said college of physicians and surgeons, and in conformity with their charter, to carry out the objects of the above resolutions.

Resolved, That the said connection shall continue during the pleasure of this board, and may be terminated by a vote of this board, and notice thereof given to the trustees of physicians and surgeons and to the regents of the university.

Resolved, That this connection shall be without prejudice to the independence of this college, and that this

---

* The words in brackets are not in the original minute. They are required by the construction, and also by the 3d of the conditions proposed in Dr. Delafield's communication.

college does not admit or recognize thereby the right of visitation in the regents of the University to any parts or institutions of Columbia college except the above school of medicine.

The regents appear to have entertained some doubt as to their competency to grant a charter in the form desired; and at the suggestion of a committee of that body the college of physicians and surgeons resorted to the legislature for such modification of their existing charter as should enable them to enter into the proposed alliance with Columbia college. An act was accordingly passed on the 24th of March, 1860, in conformity with the wishes of the petitioners.

1860, June 4. The committee of conference on the part of Columbia college reported to the board on the 4th of June, 1860, that by the action of the legislature all difficulties in the way of union had been removed; and that the joint committee of conference of the two colleges had resolved to recommend a union of the two institutions to take place on conditions embraced in the following resolutions:

Resolved, That the board of trustees of Columbia college hereby adopts the college of physicians and surgeons in the city of New York as the medical school of Columbia college.

Resolved, That the diplomas of the degree of doctor of medicine shall be conferred by the president of the college of physicians and surgeons, sitting with the president of Columbia college, and shall be signed by the presidents of the respective colleges, and such other of the faculty as may be designated from time to time by by-laws or resolutions of the college of physicians and surgeons.

Resolved, That this connection shall be continued during the pleasure of the respective boards of trustees of the two colleges, and may be determined by a vote of either board, and notice thereof given to the other board of trustees.

Whereupon the resolutions were adopted, and the college of physicians and surgeons of the city of New York became the school of medicine of Columbia college.

MERIT ROLLS.

1856, Oct. 6.   *Resolved*, That any professor of the college may, at the end of each term, prepare in printed form, a list of those students who have acquitted themselves well in his department, showing alike their *relative* and absolute scholarship, and transmit the same to the president, who shall cause the same to be sent to the parents or guardians of the students named in such list.

METEOROLOGICAL OBSERVATIONS.

1820, Nov. 18.   By resolution adopted November 18, 1820, the professor of natural and experimental philosophy and chemistry was instructed to keep a strictly accurate meteorological journal, open to the inspection of the president, professors, and trustees of the college, and any other persons by their permission; and that in the absence of such professor this duty shall devolve upon the professor of mathematics.

1865, Jan. 9.   *Resolved*, That a sum not exceeding one hundred dollars be appropriated for fitting up a room in the college, to be occupied by a person designated by the president to keep the meteorological observations.

1865, Oct. 9.   *Resolved*, That the professor of general chemistry be authorized to employ a skilled assistant in his laboratory, whose duty shall be not only to aid him in the business of his department, but also to keep the meteorological record for the college and the regents of the university, at an annual salary of five hundred dollars, to be paid on the usual college quarter-days.

MILITARY EDUCATION.

1862, Feb. 3.   A communication was received from the regents of the university suggesting the creation of a department of military instruction in the college. It was read and referred to the faculty of the college to report their views, with the request that, should they approve the proposition, they should report a scheme or plan for carrying out the design.

1862, March 3.   The president presented a report, prepared by a committee of the faculty, on the proposition to introduce military instruction into the college, which had been referred to them at the meeting of February 3. The report disapproved the proposition—first, on the score of time; secondly, because of the incongruity of the systems of military and civilian education; and thirdly, because, so far as instruction in science is concerned, the proposed plan is needless. The faculty, however, admitted the benefit which might result from a system of military drill in respect to the development and invigoration of the physical system; but suggested that the same advantages might be secured by the erection of a gymnasium, and a provision for a system of military gymnastic exercises, including the noble science of defence, boxing and fencing.

The report was adopted as expressing the sense of the board, with the exception of the part relating to a gymnasium; and it was ordered that the part so adopted be transmitted to the regents. The portion relating to a gymnasium was referred to a special committee to report.

1862, April 7.   The committee on the proposition to establish a gymnasium, and school of military exercises, boxing and fencing, reported unfavorably, but asked to be continued.

1862, Oct. 6.   The minutes make no further mention of this committee, but on the 6th October, 1862, the sum of three hundred and fifty dollars was appropriated for establishing and furnishing a fencing-room, and for the salary of a teacher for six months. Appropriations were subsequently made, January 5, 1863, and June 23, 1863, for the further payment of the teacher; and on the 5th of October, 1863, it was—

1863, Oct. 5. *Resolved*, That the president have permission, in his discretion, to employ a fencing-master for the ensuing year, on the same terms as were authorized for the past year.

In the exercise of his discretion under this resolution, the president discontinued the school of fencing after the close of the academic year ending June 29, 1864.

This was not the first time that the expediency of introducing gymnastic exercises into the college had been brought before the board; for in October, 1859, the following resolution on the subject was introduced and passed:

1859, Oct. 3. *Resolved*, That it be referred to the standing committee to examine and report as to the expediency of introducing gymnastic exercises into the college, and the probable expense thereof.

The committee appear never to have reported on the subject.

MINES, SCHOOL OF.

1863, April 1. A communication having been made in relation to a plan of Mr. Thomas Egleston, jr., for establishing a school of mines and metallurgy in connection with the college, and it having been suggested that the legislature had in contemplation a design of making a large grant of lands for the purpose of aiding scientific investigation, the subject of the expediency of establishing such school and of procuring a grant of land from the legislature was referred to a select committee, to report.

Mr. Betts, Mr. Strong, and Dr. Torrey were appointed the committee.

1863, May 4. The committee to whom it was referred to consider the expediency of establishing a school of mines and metallurgy as part of the post-graduate instruction of the college, respectfully report:

That the establishment of such school would, in their opinion, promote the interests of this college and of the community at large; but that its complete organization with the necessary apparatus, collections, &c., would require an outlay estimated at between seventeen and eighteen thousand dollars, and is therefore not expedient at the present time.

The committee are of opinion, however, that the nucleus of such school may be formed at inconsiderable cost to the college, and so as to be capable of expansion whenever the means of the college shall permit. They therefore recommend that rooms be selected and set apart for the use of such school within the present college building, that post-graduate or university professors of analytical chemistry, of mining and metallurgy, and of mineralogy and geology, and instructors in the german and french languages be appointed; such professors and instructors to be compensated wholly by fees; and that the collections and apparatus belonging to the college be used for the purposes of instruction in the school, under such regulations as will prevent any interference in the under-graduate course.

The committee beg leave further to recommend the adoption of the following resolution:

Resolved, That the recommendations of the foregoing report be approved, and that it be referred back to the committee to report the details of the proposed organization; to nominate professors and instructors in the several departments of the school; and to report what portion of the college building can most conveniently be set apart for its use, and what amount will be required to fit them up for that purpose.

The resolution, as reported, was adopted.

1863, Dec. 21. The committee remind the board that in their report of May last, they recommended the establishment of a school of mines as likely, in their opinion, to promote the interests of the college and those of the community at large, but added that the complete organization of such a school, with the necessary apparatus, collections, &c., would not be expedient at the present time.

The committee believe, however, that the nucleus of such a school may be formed at inconsiderable expense, so as to be capable of expansion hereafter. They therefore recommend that rooms be selected in the college building for a mineralogical and geological cabinet. They state further that a member of the board of trustees has already presented, as a beginning for such a cabinet, an extensive collection of minerals; and that there is also a promise of numerous valuable specimens from the Smithsonian institution in the event of a school of mines being established in this college. The committee further recommend that there be appointed a professor of mineralogy and geology in their applications to mining, without salary, but to be entitled to the fees which he may receive from his pupils. They also recommend that, in order to promote the objects herewith presented, the sum of —— dollars be appropriated to the fitting up of cases for mineralogical and geological specimens, to the payment of express charges, and for labor. Whereupon it was—

Resolved, That a professor of mineralogy and geology in their application to mining, without salary, be appointed, and that he be entitled to receive fees under regulations hereafter to be established.

Resolved, That the sum of five hundred dollars be appropriated for the purpose of fitting up cases for mineralogical and geological specimens, the payment of express charges, and labor.

Resolved, That the committee be continued, with instructions to prepare rules and regulations on the above subjects, to be submitted to this board, and to nominate to this board professors and instructors in the french and german languages, to be compensated wholly by fees.

1864, Jan. 11. *Resolved,* That the committee on a school of mines be authorized to nominate to this board a professor of mineralogy and metallurgy, and a professor of mining engineering in the proposed school of mines, in lieu of the professor of mines and metallurgy, as recommended at the last meeting of the board.

DONATION BY GEO. T. STRONG, ESQ.

1864, March 7. It appearing to the board from the proceedings of the committee on the school of mines, &c., that George T. Strong, Esq., has presented to the college a valuable collection of minerals, it was—

Resolved, That the thanks of this board be presented to Mr. Strong for his liberal gift, and that the clerk transmit to him a copy of this resolution.

DONATION FROM THE SMITHSONIAN INSTITUTION.

1864, April 4. The committee on the school of mines reported a correspondence between the committee and professor Henry of the Smithsonian institution, in which professor Henry proposes to present to the school a suite of minerals of considerable value. Thereupon it was—

Ordered, That an acknowledgment of professor Henry's letter be made, accompanied with the thanks of this board, and that the committee on a school of mines be empowered to receive the specimens.

OPENING OF THE SCHOOL.

1863, Dec. 14. *Resolved,* That the committee on the school of mines have power to advertise the opening of the school when prepared to do so.

MINES, SCHOOL OF.

INQUIRY RESPECTING GRANTS OF LAND BY CONGRESS.

1864, Sept. 14. *Resolved,* That it be referred to the committee on mines to inquire whether any grants of land have been made by congress for the benefit of scientific institutions in this state; and that they be empowered to enter into communication with the regents of the university of this state, or any body or persons having authority in the premises, with a view of ascertaining whether it is for the interest of this college to apply for the same or any part thereof; and if they deem it expedient, to make application for the same; and further, that the seal of the college may be affixed to any memorial in respect to the same, and the signatures of the chairman and the clerk of the board affixed.

DONATION BY HON. GOUVERNEUR KEMBLE.

1864, Sept. 14. *Resolved,* That the thanks of the board be presented to Mr. Gouverneur Kemble, for his liberal donation of a valuable collection of minerals; and that he be informed that arrangements are now in progress for establishing as a portion of the post-graduate instruction in the college, a school of mines and metallurgy; and that a course of lectures on mineralogy will form a necessary part of the instruction in said school.

1864, Oct. 5. *Resolved,* That the collection of minerals presented to the college by the Hon. Governeur Kemble be catalogued and arranged in cases apart from the other mineralogical collections, in honor of the gentleman to whose munificence the college is indebted for this valuable addition to its means of instruction in science.

1865, Jan. 9. *Resolved,* That the collection of minerals presented by Mr. Gouverneur Kemble, instead of being disposed of as heretofore directed, be arranged in such a way as may render it most useful to the school; and that it be catalogued with the general collection, when the same shall be done, and that the name of Mr. Kemble be placed on each specimen presented by him, and likewise be designated in the catalogue.

FURNITURE AND EQUIPMENTS.

1864, Dec. 5. *Resolved,* That the sum of two thousand two hundred and fifty dollars be appropriated for the furniture and equipments of the school of mines, and expended under the direction of the committee, and that the school be provided with light and fuel by the college.

FOREIGN CORRESPONDENCE.

Resolved, That the president and faculty be authorized to open such correspondence with schools of science in Great Britain, and on the continent of Europe, as may secure mutual intercourse and aid; and likewise with the authorities of the United States, and of this and other states and countries.

Resolved, That the clerk be authorized, under the direction of the committee, to affix the seal of the college to such communications above mentioned as may require such seal.

1866, Oct. 3. *Resolved,* That the president of the college be authorized to purchase copies of the reports of the geological surveys of the several states and territories of the United States, made under state or national authority, for presentation to the libraries of the schools of mines in Europe which have responded, or which may respond, to the invitation of the school of mines of Columbia college, to exchange publications; provided that the amount expended shall not exceed the sum of fifty dollars in case of any single school.

1867, Dec. 2. *Resolved,* That an additional appropriation of five hundred and twenty-five dollars be made for donations by the school of mines to foreign schools.

ASSOCIATES OF THE COMMITTEE.

1864, Dec. 5. *Resolved,* That until the further order of this board, the committee on the school of mines be authorized to associate with themselves, from time to time, such gentlemen interested in the development of the mineral wealth of the country as they may deem expedient, under the title "associates of the committee of the school of mines," for the purpose of aiding the committee in the establishment and development of the school.

LIBRARY.

The following resolution was adopted by the library committee, transferring certain books from the library of the college to the library of the school of mines:

Resolved, That any books in the library of the college relating to the subject of geology, mineralogy, engineering, mining, chemistry, or physics, which in the judgment of the president it may be expedient to select for the purpose, be transferred to the library of the school of mines, and placed in charge of the professor of chemistry of that school, until the further order of this committee, or of the board of trustees.

Resolved, That the said professor of chemistry be required to give his receipt for the books so transferred, and held responsible for their safe keeping and careful use, in the same manner as is the librarian of the college at present, and that said librarian be not relieved of his responsibility for the care of said books, unless and until they may be restored to the library.

Resolved, That all persons who, by the laws of the college, are entitled to the use of books belonging to the library, shall continue to enjoy that privilege in regard to the books transferred under the foregoing resolutions, in the same manner as heretofore.

Resolved, That accommodations for securely keeping and preserving from injury the books transferred as above directed, shall be provided by the school of mines, and that no such transfer shall be made until the accommodations so prepared shall have been examined and judged to be suitable by the president.

PROPOSED NEW CORPORATION.

1864, Dec. 19. *Resolved,* That it be referred to the committee on the school of mines, to inquire and report as to the expediency of organizing a new corporation, under the act of 1848, to be styled the " trustees of the school of mines," the corporators to be the members of that committee and the associates appointed under the order of the board, such corporation to have the general management of the school and to raise a fund for its endowment; it being, however, provided that no appointment to a professorship in the school or to fill vacancies among such trustees be valid till confirmed by a vote of this board; and that all apparatus, books, collections, &c., belonging to the college and now used by the school, shall continue to be the property of the college, and may be withdrawn by it at any time.

1865, Jan. 9. Under this resolution, the committee presented a report on the ninth of January, 1865; after which the subject was recommitted, with instructions to report further at the stated meeting in February. On the sixth of February, the committee reported unfavorably to the proposed plan of organization, and submitted estimates of the amount of money required to maintain the school through the current year, and through the year next ensuing. Whereupon it was—

1865, Feb. 6. *Resolved,* That a sum not exceeding three thousand dollars be appropriated for the expenses of every kind of the school of mines for the present academic year, in addition to the appropriations already made for that purpose; all the sums now and previously appropriated to be expended for the purposes to which in the report of the committee on the school of mines made this day, or in that made on the fifth day of December last, it was recommended that they should be devoted, as well as to payment of compensation to assistants for services which have been actually rendered.

Resolved, That the report be recommitted, with instructions to report specific recommendations at the next meeting of this board, for the organization and future operations of the school.

Resolved, That in the opinion of this board, the school of mines is entitled to and shall receive from this board an appropriation sufficient to ensure its continuance during the next academic year, not exceeding the minimum estimate of the committee presented this day.

PROPOSITION TO RAISE ENDOWMENT FUND.

At the ensuing meeting, the committee having reported, the following resolutions were adopted:

1865, March 6. *Whereas,* The trustees of Columbia college in the city of New York have established a school of mines in said city, and are desirous that the same should be conducted and maintained in a manner that may advance the interests of science, and in connection therewith develop the mineral recources of the country; and—

Whereas, It is deemed important that an adequate provision shall be made for this object by a sufficient endowment to reach, if possible, in means, buildings, and equipment, the sum or value of five hundred thousand dollars; and—

Whereas, It has been suggested that if the trustees be willing to contribute in lands, buildings, and money, one half of the amount, the other half can be raised and will be given to the college; now, therefore, be it—

Resolved, That, if the sum of two hundred and fifty thousand dollars be subscribed and paid toward the establishment of the school within one year from this date, the board will set apart in land or contribute in money, or partly in land and partly in money, to the value of two hundred and fifty thousand dollars, for that purpose; and further—

Resolved, That the associates of the school of mines be hereby invited and requested to co-operate in this object, under the organization proposed by the following resolutions:

Resolved, That the associates of the committee on the school of mines be authorized and requested to meet with said committee, from time to time, during its continuance, subject to the regulations hereinafter mentioned, and such other as may be hereafter adopted by the board of trustees.

Resolved, That, at any meeting of the committee, any number shall constitute a quorum, provided four trustees be present.

Resolved, That at such joint meeting, any two members may require any vote to be taken separately by the associates of the committee and by the trustees present, and that in such case a concurrence of both shall be necessary to action; but either or both may report a separate recommendation to the board of trustees.

1865, Nov. 6. A report was submitted from the committee on the school of mines, showing that the contributions received and interest allowed by the mutual life and trust company amounted to four thousand five hundred and seven dollars and three cents, and that the committee thought it expedient to postpone any attempt to raise the sum of two hundred and fifty thousand dollars (under resolution of the board heretofore adopted), until the school shall have reopened in November.

1866, March 5. *Resolved,* That the time for receiving contributions for the school of mines in conformity with the resolution heretofore passed by this board, be extended for one year.

MINES, SCHOOL OF. 99

INSTRUCTION IN RAILWAY ENGINEERING.

1865, April 3. *Resolved,* That in view of the great advantages to be derived from the co-operation of the railroad interests of the country, full instruction be given in railway engineering, as soon as the funds of the school will permit.

FREE SCHOLARSHIPS.

1865, April 3. *Resolved,* That every person or corporation subscribing the amount of five thousand dollars toward the fund for establishing and endowing the school of mines of Columbia college, shall be entitled to have one student in the school without charge for tuition fees, subject, however, to the discipline and general regulations of the school; such subscription, however, to be contingent on raising a fund of two hundred and fifty thousand dollars, independently of the college.

INSTRUCTION IN PHYSICS AND GENERAL CHEMISTRY.

1865, May 9. *Resolved,* That the board of trustees be requested to make such secure provision for instruction in pure mathematics, physics, and general chemistry in the school of mines, as to guard against the possibility of any inconvenience which might arise from the cessation of such instruction on the part of the gentlemen, or any of them, who have heretofore contributed their services voluntarily in those departments.

Committed to the president to report—report presented Oct. 9, 1865, whereupon the following resolutions were adopted:

1865, Oct. 9. *Resolved,* That instruction in the school of mines be given by professors belonging to the faculty of arts, as follows:

Instruction in physics, by professor Rood.
Instruction in general chemistry, by professor Joy.

Instruction in pure mathematics, by professor Van Amringe.

Instruction in mechanics and its applications, by professor Peck.

And that the time assigned them with their classes be such as the committee on the school may determine.

Resolved, That the title of the chair of chemistry in the school of mines be so altered that it shall be hereafter called the chair of analytical and applied chemistry.

Resolved, That the professors in the faculty of arts who give instruction, under the resolutions of this board, in the school of mines, be entitled to seats in the faculty of the said school, as members of the same, and be styled professors in the school.

ENLARGEMENT OF THE SCHOOL.

1865, May 3. *Resolved*, That the sum of one thousand dollars be appropriated to fitting up the building formerly used as a paper manufactory, for the use of the school of mines; and that the amount be paid under the direction of the treasurer.

SUPPORT OF THE SCHOOL.

1865, June 5. *Resolved*, That the following appropriations be made for the support of the school of mines until the end of the next financial year, to wit, until 30th September, 1866:

First, for salaries, as follows:

Professor of chemistry for the next financial year.	$3,000
Professor of mineralogy and metallurgy	3,000
Professor of mining engineering	3,000
Two assistants in chemistry	1,000
One assistant in drawing	500
A janitor, per annum	500

The salaries above mentioned shall be payable as follows: of the professors and their assistants in four equal payments to be made on the fifteenth day of each of the months of November, February, May and June, after the commencement of the next financial year; of the janitor in equal monthly payments to be made on the first day of each month after this day, until and including 1st October, 1866.

Second, for general expenses :

Supplies	$625
Printing and advertising	500
Fitting up of building heretofore appropriated	1,000

Third, for the department of instruction :

Chemical department—chemicals, $2,000 ; fixtures, $4,000 ; perishable apparatus, $2,500	$8,500
Department of drawing—models, $200 ; fixtures, $150 ; students' supplies, $150	500
Department of mining engineering— diagrams, $100 ; models, $50	150
Department of metallurgy —diagrams, $250 ; models, $300	550
Department of mineralogy—diagrams, $100 ; models, $100 ; minerals, 300 ; cases and drawers, $3,000 ; contingent expenses, $300	3,800
Department of geology—maps and diagrams, $250 ; specimens, $300 ; cases and drawers, $150 ; contingent expenses $150	850

1865, Oct. 9. *Resolved*, That an additional appropriation of $325 be made for fitting up the school of mines.

CONTROL OF EXPENDITURES.

1865, June 5. All expenditures for general expenses shall be made under the direction of the president, and the bills for the same shall be certified by him to be correct before the same shall be paid.

The expenditures for each department of instruction shall be made by the professor having charge of such department, and shall not exceed the appropriation therefor. The bills for such expenditure shall be certified by the professor to be correct before the same shall be paid. All fees received from students attending the mining school, shall be paid to the treasurer from time to time as the same shall be collected.

1866, Oct. 3. *Resolved*, That immediately after the termination of the financial year, the professor of analytical and applied chemistry shall submit to the treasurer his accounts of apparatus furnished to the students, and returned or broken by them, with the amounts paid for apparatus broken, and that the same be audited by the standing committee.

1868, March 2. *Resolved*, That the dean of the faculty of the school of mines be required to report to the treasurer from time to time, at the convenience of the treasurer, the amount of the receipts from students in the chemical laboratory for breakage and supplies, and that the same be added to the appropriation for the department of analytical chemistry, to be expended under the regulations which govern the expenditures of that appropriation.

DEAN OF THE FACULTY.

1865, Oct. 9. *Resolved*, That the statute organizing the school of mines be amended by introducing the following section immediately after sec. 4, chap. 2 :

"Sec. 5. The faculty of the school shall be authorized to elect a dean from their own number, who shall be charged with such duties as the president may delegate to him."

And that the subsequent sections be numbered accordingly.

1865, Dec. 4. *Resolved*, That it be referred to the standing committee to devise some mode by which the dean of the faculty of the school of mines may be relieved from the expense which he is called upon to meet for express and other charges imposed on him from time to time, and that they report thereon.

1865, Dec. 18. *Resolved*, That the treasurer be authorized to advance from time to time to the dean of the faculty of the school of mines a sum not to exceed three hundred dollars, to be applied by him to the payment of such expenses of the school as convenience may require to be paid without in the first instance sending the bills to the treasurer for payment.

DAMAGE TO APPARATUS.

1865, Oct. 9. *Resolved*, That the moneys received from students on account of apparatus broken be retained by the professor and applied by him to the purchase of new apparatus.

1867, Nov. 4. *Resolved*, That there be added to section 22d of the by-laws of the school of mines the following, viz. :

"A deposit of five dollars will be required from each student using any collection, and at the end of each session any damage done to such collection must be paid for by the student committing the damage, or, if he cannot be discovered, will be deducted from the aggregate deposit of all the students."

TERMS OF INSTRUCTION.

1865, Oct. 9. *Resolved*, That the terms of instruction in the school of mines shall, after the present year, begin and end on the same days on which the terms in the collegiate department begin and end ; and that the term for the present year shall extend until the close of the collegiate year.

VACATIONS.

1865, Dec. 18.   *Resolved,* That there be a short winter vacation in the school of mines, immediately following the close of the studies of the first session in the academical department, and ending for first year students when the second college session commences; and for the second and third year students on the Wednesday nearest the first day of March; such vacation to be employed by the two higher classes as the rules of the school of mines may require. Modified November 5, 1866.

1866, Nov. 5.   *Ordered,* That the winter vacation of the school of mines be abolished, and that the exercises of the school be discontinued only during that portion of the year in which the regular academic exercises are suspended.

1867, Dec. 2.   *Resolved,* That the paragraph relating to the winter vacation be stricken from the resolutions for the government of the school of mines.

DEGREES IN THE SCHOOL OF MINES.

1866, April 2.   The president read the following as a report from the faculty of the school of mines:

NEW YORK, *March* 22, 1866.

At a meeting of the faculty of the school of mines, held this day, president Barnard in the chair, the following resolutions were adopted:

The board of trustees having referred to this faculty the question, what degrees ought to be conferred upon proficient students in the school of mines, and what should be the conditions on which such degrees should be granted, be it therefore—

Resolved, That the course of study now required to be pursued by the regular classes in the school, and which is set forth in detail in the published circulars, is intended to be, and is believed actually to be, fully equivalent to that which is required for the degree of engineer of mines in foreign schools of the same character; and that, therefore, in the opinion of this faculty, all the students who shall have pursued that course to the end, and shall have passed satisfactory examinations upon the several studies embraced in it, are fairly entitled to receive, and accordingly ought to receive, the degree of engineer of mines; provided that the studies of french and german and botany shall not be held to be obligatory parts of this course.

Resolved, That it is customary in schools of science, both in this country and abroad, to confer the degree of bachelor of philosophy upon students who pass approved examinations upon certain groups of studies considered to be sufficient to justify such a distinction, and that therefore all students in this school who shall have passed such approved examinations upon the studies of either of the following groups, viz.:

GROUP I.—Analytical geometry, calculus, descriptive geometry, drawing, mechanics, physics, inorganic chemistry, mineralogy, geology, conservation of force, and connection of the sciences:

GROUP II.—Physics, inorganic chemistry, stoichiometry, analytical chemistry (qualitative and quantitative), assaying, mineralogy, geology, palæontology, and botany—

Are, in the opinion of this faculty, entitled to receive the degree of bachelor of philosophy.

Resolved, That the degree of doctor of philosophy ought to be conferred in cases of pre-eminent merit and large acquisition, and that it should be left to the faculty of the school of mines to decide in what cases this degree should be given.

The report was accepted, and its consideration postponed to the next meeting of the board, but no action upon it was ever taken.

ERECTION OF BUILDING.

1866, May 7.   By resolution of this date, an appropriation of fifteen thousand dollars was made for the erection of a temporary building on the college ground for the use of the school of mines, and for the furnishing of the same. The committee on the school was authorized to contract for the same.

1866, June 12.   *Resolved,* That in lieu of the appropriation of fifteen thousand dollars made at a former meeting of this board for the erection of a building for the school of mines, a sum not exceeding thirty-five thousand dollars be appropriated to defray the cost of such building and of the alterations which may be necessary in the old building, and also of the fixtures, apparatus, and outfit required to put the school into operation upon its enlarged scale.

ASSISTANTS.

1866, June 12.   *Resolved,* That until the further order of this board, the professor of analytical and applied chemistry in the school of mines be authorized to employ two assistants in chemical analysis at salaries of one thousand dollars per annum, and one assistant in analysis, and one assistant in assaying, at salaries of five hundred dollars per annum; also, that the professor of mining engineering be authorized to employ one assistant at a salary of one thousand dollars per annum, and the professor of mineralogy one assistant at a salary of five hundred dollars per annum.

1868, April 6.   *Resolved,* That the president be, and he hereby is, authorized to appoint as honorary assistants without compensation, in those departments in the school of mines in which such assistants can be of use, any meritorious students whom he may deem to be deserving of the distinction; such appointments to be made with the consent and on the recommendation of the several professors in those departments, and to be employed as incentives to diligence, as rewards of merit, and for the purpose of increasing the efficiency of the departments.

Resolved, That the professor of geology and palæontology be authorized to appoint, subject to the approval of the president, an assistant in his department at a salary of five hundred dollars a year.

REGISTRAR.

1866, June 12. *Resolved*, That the dean of the faculty of the school of mines be authorized to appoint, with the approval of the president, a suitable person to serve as registrar and librarian of the school until the further order of this board, at the annual salary of one thousand dollars.

GEOLOGICAL COLLECTION.

1866, Nov. 26. *Ordered*, That three thousand three hundred dollars be appropriated for the purchase of cases for the geological collection of the school of mines.

1867, March 4. An addition of ninety-five dollars was made by resolution of this date to the appropriation in the foregoing resolution.

1868, April 6. *Resolved*, That a committee of three be appointed to inquire and report to this board whether any arrangement can be made by which the geological collection belonging to Dr. Newberry can be acquired for the college; and that the same committee make a similar inquiry and report in regard to the mineralogical collection of professor Egleston.

GRATUITOUS INSTRUCTION.

1867, Nov. 4. *Resolved*, That the graduates of the school of mines shall have the privilege of attending the lectures of the school without charge for tuition.

1868, June 1. By resolution of this date, the president is authorized, in his discretion, to permit *any* student who shall have pursued a *regular course* in the school for three years, and shall have paid his fees for the same, to continue afterwards to attend without charge.

PLAN OF INSTRUCTION.

1868, April 6. A communication was received from the faculty of the school of mines, proposing that the period of instruction be extended from three years to four years; and that there be established five parallel courses of instruction to occupy the third and fourth years—all the students during the first and second years to pursue one common course; that the five parallel courses be distinguished by the names, "mining engineering," "civil engineering," "metallurgy," "geology and natural history," and "analytical and applied chemistry;" and finally, that there be conferred on students who shall successfully complete the first and third courses the degree of "mining engineer;" on those who, in like manner, complete the second, the degree of "civil engineer;" and on those who complete either of the remaining two, in like manner, the degree of "bachelor of philosophy." The communication was referred to the committee on the school of mines, to report at the next meeting of the board.

1868, May 4. The committee on the school of mines reported in favor of adopting, in substance, the plan for the course of instruction proposed by the faculty of the school; but suggested a modification in form. They recommended that all the studies laid down in the plan as studies of the first year, with the exception of french, german, and drawing, be made requisitions for admission to the school; and that the regular studies of the school should be completed in three years, and should be those laid down in the plan for the second, third, and fourth years. And for the accommodation of any who might desire special facilities for preparing themselves to enter the school, they recommended that there should be established a preparatory course to continue one year, and to embrace the studies included within the plan for the first year. They recommended, finally, that the years distinguished as second, third, and fourth in the plan, be called first, second, and third, and that graduation take place at the end of the third year.

Resolutions embodying these recommendations were presented, and after discussion were adopted.

MINUTES OF THE BOARD.

1857, Jan. 5. At a stated meeting of the board held on this day, the clerk communicated to the board a demand, made on behalf of the regents of the university, by letter from E. C. Benedict, their secretary, for the original minutes of the board from 1784 to 1787. It was resolved that the subject be referred to a special committee.

1857, Feb. 2. The special committee to whom the demand of the regents of the university for the original minutes of the board, from 1784 to 1787, was referred, reported that the right to the original minutes is vested in the trustees of Columbia college, and it was—

Resolved, That the report be adopted; that the committee reply to the communication of Mr. Benedict; that they likewise transmit to the regents of the university a copy of the report, and furnish the regents with a copy of the minutes, extending from 1784 to 1787.

1860, Jan. 9. *Resolved*, That the minutes of the trustees, from their commencement to the time of transcribing, be transcribed under the direction of the clerk, in proper books to be provided by him for that purpose, and that he be empowered from time to time to call on the treasurer for the payment of the expenses attending such transcription, at an expense not exceeding three hundred dollars.

Resolved, That a safe be provided for the records of the college in the custody of the clerk, and likewise a desk for filing the papers directed to be filed, and that said papers be marked and indexed; likewise that the treasurer be authorized to pay for such safe and desk.

MODERN LANGUAGES.

1843, July 24. *Resolved,* That the german language and literature be made a part of the sub-graduate course.

1847, Jan. 4. *Resolved,* 1st. That henceforth such members of the senior and junior classes as shall choose to continue their attendance on the Gebhard professor, be at liberty to do so under such regulations as may be established by the president; and that the professor deliver his instructions to them at the hours now appropriated to those classes respectively, or at such other convenient hours as may hereafter be assigned.

A second resolution, that the present sophomore class be required to attend german two days a week, was subsequently repealed.

1857, Dec. 7. *Resolved,* That in conformity with the scheme reported in relation to instruction in the german language, &c., two prizes for the german, one of thirty dollars, the other for twenty dollars, be awarded annually to the best students in each of the two classes into which it is proposed to divide the students: provided that—

In every case, the award be made to those among the competitors in each class sustaining the best examination. The decision to rest with the professor of the department and the president.

1858, Feb. 1. *Resolved,* That whenever it shall be deemed expedient by the trustees to organize classes in french and spanish, they should be organized in two classes, and two hours of instruction a week be given to each class; the students to proceed from the lower to the higher class on examination; and the course of instruction to be left to the discretion of the several professors, subject to the direction of the trustees.

NATURAL HISTORY, LYCEUM OF.

1865, Jan. 23. On January 23, 1865, it was resolved that the two rooms in the college building heretofore occupied by the college chemical society be tendered to the New York Lyceum of natural history for their meetings and for the accommodation of their collections, if the same be found to be adapted to their purposes.

OBSERVATORY, ASTRONOMICAL.

Whereas, Measures have been set on foot by the alumni and other friends of the college, for erecting and establishing an astronomical observatory in, or in the vicinity of, this city, and of placing the same under the superintendence of this board;

1846, April 6. *Resolved,* That a committee consisting of three persons be appointed to inquire into the subject and to report what measures have been taken, and what action of the board, if any, is necessary or expedient in the matter.

Whereupon, Messrs. Betts, Fish, and Lawrence were appointed the committee.

1857, June 29. A communication from professor Hackley, asking an appropriation of one thousand dollars for an astronomical observatory, was referred to the building committee with power.

1858, June 2. *Resolved,* That the committee to which it was heretofore referred to select and obtain a site for an astronomical observatory, be discharged from the further consideration of that subject, and that the same be referred to a select committee of three.

Mr. Rutherfurd, Dr. Torrey, and Dr. Anderson, were appointed such committee.

The committee on the astronomical observatory having reported that a suitable site for such building had been found in central park, it was—

1859, Jan. 3. *Resolved,* That it be referred to the same committee to take such measures as they may deem advisable, to procure a right to a site for an observatory in the central park.

1859, Feb. 7. *Resolved,* That the committee appointed to procure a site in the central park for an astronomical observatory, be requested to discontinue their action for the present.

PRESIDENT, OF THE.

1832, Nov. 11. *Resolved,* That it be the duty of the president to report to this board at each stated meeting after the first Monday in December in each collegiate year, the names of the parents and guardians who shall have failed to pay the tuition fees of their children or wards.

1846, June 1. *Resolved,* That it be the duty of the president to make return quarterly to this board, of the attendance of the members of the faculty of the college at the daily prayers and exercises in the chapel, and at the public examinations and exhibitions, according to the requirements of the statutes, chapter i., § 7, and chapter ix., § 3, and that the clerk communicate this resolution to the board of the college.

1864, June 6. *Resolved,* That a sum not exceeding three thousand dollars be appropriated, to enable Dr. Barnard to furnish the president's house, the amount expended to be applied by him with the approbation of the treasurer; the furniture to be the property of the college.

1864, Sept. 14. *Resolved,* That the president be empowered to appoint a secretary, at a salary of five hundred dollars per annum, during the pleasure of this board.

Resolved, That the duty of instruction in the evidences of natural and revealed religion be entrusted to the president of the college.

PRIZE SCHOLARSHIPS AND PRIZES.

1843, June 5.   1*st. Resolved,* That the trustees of Columbia college agree to and do hereby accept the terms offered by the society for promoting religion and learning in the state of New York, and the scholarship placed at their disposal by the said society, on the conditions hereunto annexed.

2*d. Resolved,* That a certified copy of the above resolution, annexed to a copy of the conditions therein referred to, be transmitted to the chairman of the education committee of the above-named society.

3*d. Resolved,* That until some permanent arrangement as regards the said scholarship shall by statute have been made, the president be empowered to take such steps as may be necessary in order to render it open to candidates from the present senior class.

The conditions above referred to are as follows:

1. Such nominee to be of the age and other conditions requisite to his entrance in the general theological seminary, and as candidate in the protestant episcopal church.

2. That he shall have completed his college course, taken his degree of A. B., and been enrolled among those receiving special honors on quitting the college.

3. That he shall have carried off the prize in question, viz.: the seminary scholarship in open competition, under the judgment of the faculty, from his classmates competing for it. All competitors to report themselves to the education committee of the society at least three months previous to the trial.

4th. That such scholarship be held during good behavior, subject to the society rules and regulations for its scholars.

5th. That in return for such rights of annual nomination to a seminary scholarship entitling the nominee to the full seminary course (now of three years) without charge and with an annual stipend of two hundred dollars, the college to grant free tuition to two annual nominees of the society, entitling them in like manner to the full college course of four years—in other words, to two free students in each class.

1852, March 1. The president presented the following scheme :

"Scheme of two annual seminary prizes, founded by the Rev. John McVickar, D.D., through the society for promoting religion and learning, &c. (in Columbia college), and for which an endowment of $1,000 is herewith provided, on the following conditions :

"*1st.* The first to be entitled the society's greek seminary prize of thirty dollars, to be annually competed for among such members of the graduating class as shall have given in their names to the president at least one month previous to such competition, as candidates for the general theological seminary of the protestant episcopal church.

"The examination for such prize to be held publicly in the chapel, and separate from the general college examinations.

"1. The epistles of the new testament in greek "*ad aperturam libri.*"

"2. On some of the early greek fathers, to be designated at the time of noticing the prize; or if none be designated, then upon some portion of Chrysostom or Athanasius, at the choice of the student. The decision to be with the president or greek professor in the same manner as the other special college testimonials are decided.

"2d. The second to be entitled the society's english seminary prize of twenty dollars, to be annually competed for as before, and to consist in the production of an essay (to be publicly read or not as the president may determine) of the ordinary length of a public discourse, on some subject connected with the course of evidences, and given out by him at the time of notice; and the prize to be adjudged as before by the president and professor of that branch. Such discussion to have respect to—

"1. The general ability and soundness of the essay.

"2. Its logical and demonstrative form.

"3. The pure saxon style and idiom in which it is written.

"Notice of the above prizes with their conditions to be publicly given out in the chapel each year at the commencement of the closing term of the senior class, and each student giving in his name as 'competitor' to designate the prize for which he contends, and to be confined to the choice then made.

"The names of the successful candidates in both prizes to be enrolled in a suitable book to be provided and kept for that purpose, lettered appropriately and kept on the library table, and also to be announced with other honors on commencement day.

"Payment of the above prizes to be made by the treasurer of the society on certificate of the president of the name of the successful candidate, and the fulfilment of the prescribed conditions; the same being inclosed in a personal letter from the candidate himself, stating his intention of entering the seminary at the opening of the ensuing term; and such payment not be taken into account in the payment of any stipend allowed to such scholar on the part of the society itself. The names of the successful candidates to be also recorded honorably on the society's books.

"In case of lapse on the part of the college in the bestowment of one or both prizes, then the amount of such prize or prizes is not to pass into the general funds of the society, but to be specially appropriated by the members of the board in such manner as they may deem best for furthering the end designed by this endowment, viz.: that of enlarging the numbers and advancing the scholarship of candidates for the ministry within the general theological seminary of our church, educated in Columbia college."

Resolved, That the proposition contained in such scheme be adopted.

1857, Dec. 2

Resolved, That, in conformity with the scheme reported in relation to instruction in the german language, &c., two prizes for the german, one of thirty dollars, the other of twenty dollars, be awarded annually to the best student in each of the two classes into which it is proposed to divide the students; provided that, in every case, the award be made to those among the competitors in each class sustaining the best examination, the decision to rest with the professor of the department and the president.

1858, March 1.

A communication was received from the association of the alumni of the college proposing to establish prizes to be given at commencement, and asking a conference with a committee of the trustees. Mr. Zabriskie, Mr. Jones, and Mr. Ogden were accordingly appointed as a committee of conference. This committee seems not to have reported; but the conference is presumed to have resulted in the establishment of the alumni prize to " the most faithful and deserving student of each graduating class."

1861, June 24.

Resolved, That the semi-annual exhibition and the award of prizes for excellence in declamation be discontinued.

1867, Nov. 4.

The Committee appointed to report resolutions, &c., on occasion of the death of Dr. King and professor Anthon, recommended, as a mark of esteem for the late professor, that a greek prize scholarship of the value of three hundred dollars per annum be established, to be competed for at the end of the junior year.

The recommendation was referred to said committee to report a plan and details to the trustees.

1867, Dec. 2. *Resolved*, That it be referred to the committee having charge of the resolution respecting a greek prize, to report a plan for a second prize of less value.

1868, May 4. The committee on the foregoing resolutions reported in favor of establishing two prizes, to be called the first prize in greek, and the second prize in greek, respectively—the first prize to be of the value of three hundred dollars, and the second prize of the value of one hundred and fifty dollars. They reported also a scheme of regulations embracing the conditions under which said prizes should be awarded. The report was accepted, and the prizes were established of the amounts and with the conditions recommended.

PROFESSORSHIPS AND PROFESSORS.

1823, Nov. 8. *Resolved*, That a professorship of law be established in this college, and that the professor be not obliged to attend the meeting of the faculty of arts, nor bound by the provisions of chapter ii. of the statutes, nor those of § 9, chapter iii.

Resolved, That the board reserves to itself the right to make such regulations in relation to said professorship, and the gentlemen attending the professor, as they may deem proper at any time hereafter.

1830, Feb. 3. *Resolved*, That the title of the adjunct professor of languages hereafter be " the Jay professor of the greek and latin languages."

1831, April 5. It was resolved that the board require as many of the classes to attend the professors four hours daily as the course of study prescribed by the statutes will allow, the hours of instruction to be as equally as may be distributed among the several professors. Also, that to the studies of the sophomore year, there be added a course of elementary chemistry.

1833, April 2. Resolutions of this date assigned to the professor of moral philosophy the duty of giving instruction in the evidences of christianity and in logic, and directed that the tutor having charge of the sophomore and freshman classes in rhetoric and belles-lettres should be under the immediate direction of the president; also, that the president give instruction to the senior class in the constitutional law of the United States.

A professorship of chemistry was at the same time added to the faculty of arts, at a salary of one thousand dollars, with a provision that the same should not be increased, the professor not to be subject to the provisions of the statutes which exact of officers other duties than those of instruction. At a subsequent meeting of the board, held May 17th, it was provided that the professor of chemistry should not be a member of the board of the college.

1857, May 18. *Resolved*, That the professors to be appointed to the several vacant chairs, viz. : of chemistry, of mathematics, of moral and intellectual philosophy, of ancient and modern literature, and of history and political economy, shall severally receive during the pleasure of the board a salary at the rate of three thousand dollars per annum ; and in addition to such salary there shall be allowed to those of them to whom a dwelling shall not be assigned by the college, a sum not exceeding one thousand dollars for house-rent. They shall severally conduct the studies of the sub-graduate course appropriate to their departments as such studies are or may from time to time be prescribed by the statutes of the college, and shall also take such part in the university course of studies as may be assigned to them under such arrangements and directions as shall hereafter be prescribed.

Resolved, That the salaries shall take effect from the opening of the next session.

1857, June 8. The name of the professorship of history and political economy was changed to that of history and political science.

1857, Oct. 5. The chairs of moral and intellectual philosophy and of ancient and modern literature were united, and the duties of the same assigned to one professor, under the title of professor of moral and intellectual philosophy and literature. By a resolution of the same date, the subjects of instruction were assigned to the several professors as follows:

Evidences of religion, to professor McVickar.

Greek language and literature, to professor Anthon.

Astronomy, to professor Hackley.

Latin language and literature, to professor Drisler.

Ancient history and geography, greek and roman antiquities, to professor Schmidt.

Mechanics, physics, and technology and history of the sciences under his charge, to professor McCulloh.

Modern history, political science, natural and international law, civil and common law, to professor Lieber.

Chemistry and chemical technology, geology, mining and metallurgy and natural history, *i. e.,* animal and vegetable physiology, taught in connection with organic chemistry, to professor Joy.

Mathematics, civil engineering, drawing and the history of mathematics, to professors Davies and Peck.

English composition, æsthetics, rhetoric, logic, english literature and the literature of modern Europe, intellectual and moral philosophy and the history of philosophy, to the professor of moral and intellectual philosophy and literature.

1858, Feb. 1. It was resolved that instruction in drawing be committed to the charge of the adjunct professor of mathematics.

1859, May 2. The adjunct professor of mathematics was made professor of pure mathematics; and the professor of mathematics was made professor of higher mathematics, the former with a salary of four thousand dollars, and the latter (teaching but one term in the year) at a salary of two thousand dollars per annum.

1863, Oct. 15. *Whereas*, Richard S. McCulloh, professor of mechanics and physics in this college, has abandoned his post of duty and gone to the city of Richmond and allied himself to those now in rebellion against the government of the United States; therefore—

Resolved, That the said Richard S. McCulloh be, and he hereby is, expelled from the professorship of mechanics and physics, and that the said professorship be and is hereby declared vacant.

Resolved, That the name of Richard S. McCulloh be stricken from the list of professors of this college, and that in future editions of the catalogue of this college a note stating the fact and ground of his expulsion be appended to his name.

Resolved, That a copy of the foregoing proceedings in this case be published in the daily papers in this city, be read by the president to the faculty and the students of the several departments of the college, and entered in the record-book of the board of the college.

Resolved, That the communication of professor McCulloh be filed without being entered in the minutes of the college.

1864, Jan. 11. *Resolved*, That the professor of municipal law be requested to adopt some regulations which will prevent the interruption of the meetings of the board of trustees by the entrance of students or other persons into their room

PROFESSORSHIPS AND PROFESSORS. 121

during their session; and that the clerk furnish a copy of the preceding resolution to the professor.

1864, Sept. 14. *Resolved,* That the professor of higher mathematics be requested to deliver to the junior class in the three hours per week allotted to his department in the first session, a course of lectures on the history, philosophy, and methods of mathematics, with such practical illustrations and exercises as may be necessary to make the subject intelligible.

1865, June 5. It was referred to a committee of five to consider and report on the expediency of abolishing the professorship of history, and the professorship of higher mathematics; and also, that in case the committee should deem it best for any reason, to abolish said professorships, or either of them, they should report a plan for giving of the instruction now given in those departments. The committee reported, July 3, in favor of abolishing both professorships, but the adoption of the resolutions to that effect was rendered unnecessary, by the resignation, September 14, of the professor of higher mathematics and the transfer of the professor of history to the school of law; his duties in the college being entrusted to the professor of philosophy and english literature, assisted by a tutor.

1866, June 12. *Resolved,* That the chair of french be discontinued.

PROFESSORS, EXTRA COLLEGIATE OCCUPATIONS OF.

1850, Oct. 2. By resolution passed on this date the president was directed to report whether any of the members of the board whose salaries are paid out of the general fund of the college are, or have been, within the last year, engaged in any professional pursuits from which they derive emolument, and which are not connected with the college, and if any, which of them, and for what time, and the nature of the pursuit.

1854, Nov. 6. In accordance with the above, the president having reported that professor McVickar was employed as chaplain in the United States army, and professors Anthon and Drisler in the grammar school, and that they received emolument therefor, the following resolution was moved, but consideration of it was deferred:

Resolved, That the requirements of § 2 of chap. ii. of the statutes be enforced by the college, and that a copy of this resolution be given by the clerk to each of the professors.

1854, Dec. 4. A letter having been received from professor McVickar, in explanation of the nature of his services rendered in contravention of college statutes, it was moved that the whole subject be referred to a committee of three, of which senator Fish should be chairman. In view of senator Fish's absence it was resolved that the consideration of the resolution should be postponed to the stated meeting in April next.

1855, Oct. 2. The resolution of November 6, 1854, in relation to § 2, chap. ii. of the statutes, having been called up, it was referred to the select committee — Messrs. Ogden, Betts, Bradford, Allen, and Anderson — appointed the same day as a committee of inquiry into the state of the college generally.

The minutes do not show in what manner the subject was finally disposed of.

1856, Nov. 17. *Resolved*, That after the first day of July, 1857, the statute requiring that the members of the board of the college whose salaries are paid out of the general fund of the college shall not be engaged in any professional pursuits from which they derive emoluments, and which are not connected with the college, shall be binding upon professor Drisler, notwithstanding any license or dispensation which has heretofore been granted to him by the trustees.

1860, Feb. 6. The president was requested to report to this board at its next stated meeting whether instruction is given by any of the professors to any undergraduates, other than such as is prescribed by the regular college course, and under what circumstances such instruction is given.

1860, April 2. In answer to the resolution of inquiry as to whether instruction is given by any of the professors of the college to any undergratuates, &c., the president reports that three undergraduates do attend the professor of chemistry after college hours; but that no other professor gives any instruction other than such as is prescribed by the regular college course.

No action was taken on the report.

EMERITUS PROFESSORS.

1853, Nov. 1. *Resolved*, That, for the purpose of appropriately acknowledging the services of such professors of this institution as shall have devoted themselves for a sufficient length of time—not less than twenty years—to the duties of their respective departments of instruction, there be created an order of "emeritus professorships," without salaries or stated duties, but with the following privileges and honors:

1*st*. That the name and title of emeritus professor be inserted in the printed lists of the faculties of the college.

2*d*. That the professor be regularly and officially invited to be present with the board of the college at all public examinations, processions, and celebrations.

3*d*. That he have an untransferable right of nomination to one free scholarship, to be distinguished by the name of the professor.

4*th*. That his portrait be provided at the expense of the college, and be hung on the walls of the library, or other suitable room in one of the college edifices.

5*th*. That he have gratuitous access, at the appointed times, to all the privileges of the libraries and collections.

6th. That the use of the college chapel (or, in the event of the removal of the college buildings, some equivalent facility) be afforded to the professor, for the delivery of an annual lecture, on any subject within the scope of his department, in case he should desire to avail himself of such accommodations.

1865, Sept. 25. *Resolved,* That in consideration of the valuable services rendered to the college by Charles Davies, LL. D., during the eight years in which he has been professor, and in view of his eminent attainments in mathematics, and his great ability as an instructor, he be appointed emeritus professor of mathematics in Columbia college, to hold the said office during the pleasure of the board of trustees, subject to the regulations of the board.

Resolved, That any regulation of the board heretofore adopted in relation to the office of emeritus professor, touching the number of years during which a professor shall have occupied his chair, inconsistent with the foregoing resolution, be suspended in the case of professor Davies.

1865, Nov. 5. *Resolved,* That it be referred to a special committee of five to consider and report what measures it may be necessary for this board to adopt under existing regulations in reference to the emeritus professors of this college, and also what appropriation it may be expedient to make to carry out said measures.

Resolved, That it be referred to the same committee to report whether it is expedient for this board to admit to the position of an emeritus professor of the college, any former professor thereof.

The following trustees were named as the committee: The Rev. Dr. Haight, Rev. Dr. Barnard, Mr. Betts, Mr. Ruggles, and the Rev. Dr. Hutton.

1866, Jan. 2. *Resolved,* That Dr. Henry J. Anderson, in view of his eighteen years' most valuable and acceptable services as a professor in this college, be appointed and hereby is declared to be so appointed, emeritus professor of mathematics and astronomy.

2. *Resolved*, That the several emeritus professors, Drs. McVickar, Anderson, and Davies, be informed by the president of the rights and privileges attached to their offices, and that the president request them in the name of this board to sit for their portraits, to be placed in the library of the college.

3. *Resolved*, That a committee of five be appointed to procure the several portraits to be painted, and that they be authorized to draw upon the treasurer in payment for the same a sum not exceeding one thousand dollars.

1866, March 2. *Resolved*, That when the portraits of the emeritus professors are completed, the committee having charge of the same, be authorized to adopt such measures for their formal introduction into the college as they may deem expedient.

READING-ROOM.

1867, April 1. An application was made to the trustees to authorize the fitting up of a room in the college building with tables, chairs, and other conveniences, to serve as a reading-room and place of resort for the professors and other officers of instruction in the college. The standing committee was authorized to make the provision asked for in this application.

REPAIRS.

1820, Sept. 20. A resolution of this date provided that a committee of repairs be annually appointed, who shall have power to direct all necessary repairs to the college buildings and grounds to be made, and to draw on the treasurer from time to time for the requisite sums to defray the expenses of the same, and who shall report their proceedings to this board.

1820, June 4. A resolution was passed which ordered that repairs, painting, papering, &c., of houses, in the college, occupied by the president or either of the professors, should 1826, March 6. be made at their own expense; and on March 6, 1826, it was resolved that all expenses—painting, glazing, interior work of all kinds, repairs of drains, and other repairs not expressly authorized by the board, appertaining to the houses of the president and professors, be chargeable to the occupants and not to the college.

1833, May 1. *Resolved*, That all repairs of the houses of the president and professors, excepting such as may be necessary to protect the college buildings from the effect of the weather, and also all expenditures required for the domestic accommodation of professors in and about their several houses, be hereafter made at their own charges respectively.

REVIEWS OF STUDIES.

1856, Oct. 6 *Resolved*, That the review of the studies of any term may be conducted by any professor at such times and in such order as he may judge best calculated to fix the knowledge of the students, or secure their continued attention, subject to the approval of the president. Provided, however, that the whole time consumed in making such review shall not in any department exceed the term of four weeks.

SALARIES.

1843, July 24. By resolution of this date it was ordered that, in addition to the residences for the president and the four principal professors of the college, fourteen hundred dollars a year be allowed to the president and twelve hundred to each of these professors, and also that they receive, for every student who actually pays his fees, the sum of ten dollars each. Also that the salary of the treasurer be reduced to four hundred dollars; that the system of awarding medals be abolished; and that the library expenditures shall not exceed one hundred dollars per annum. This last clause was changed by resolution
1846, June 1. of June 1, 1846, and one hundred dollars was restored to the salary of the treasurer.

1852, Dec. 13. *Resolved*, That the salary of the librarian be raised to three hundred dollars a year, to commence on the first of October last.

1856, Nov. 17. *Resolved*, That it be referred to the committee of inquiry to inquire and report what salaries ought to be paid to such professors as may reside in the college building, and to such professors as may reside elsewhere; and whether the present system of making the amount of the compensation of the professors to depend in part upon the fees of students received by the college ought to be changed or modified.

1857, May 25 *Resolved*, That from and after the first day of October next the yearly salaries appropriated to the several officers and others connected with the college shall be payable in four equal payments on the fifteenth day of February, May, June, and November, respectively, in each year.

1857, June 22. It was in 1857, June 22, resolved that the president's salary be three thousand five hundred dollars a year; that the professor of greek, of latin, of physics, and of astronomy, shall severally receive a salary at the rate of three thousand dollars per annum, and to those to whom a dwelling shall not be assigned, a sum not exceeding one thousand dollars shall be paid. The professors shall conduct the studies of the university course, as well as those of the sub-graduate course, without further compensation; all this to take effect from January 1, 1857. The amounts already received since that date shall be deducted. Fees hitherto payable by students for diploma fees are hereby abolished, and neither the president nor any of the professors are entitled to receive any portion of the tuition fees.

Resolved, That when any professor who would, under the existing regulations of the board, be entitled to an allowance for rent, shall occupy his own house, the treasurer shall be authorized to pay to such professor such an amount, as an equivalent therefor, as the standing committee may determine to be just and reasonable.

1858, June 21. By a resolution of June 21, 1858, the salary of the professor of mathematics was placed at three thousand dollars, with an allowance not exceeding one thousand dollars for house-rent; and the salary of the adjunct professor of mathematics at two thousand dollars, to be paid at the usual periods, during the pleasure of the board.

1860, Nov. 5. *Resolved*, That the salary of the treasurer be three thousand dollars per annum, to be computed and take effect from the fifteenth day of May last.

1861, June 24. A resolution of June 24, 1861, reduced the salaries of the officers of the college, to date from October 1, 1861, and the following were paid till 1864:

President	$2,800	Prof. Schmidt	$1,620
President's clerk	500	" McVickar	1,000
Prof. Anthon, and allowance of house-rent	3,600	" Davies	1,800
		Mr. Van Amringe, tutor	1,000
Prof. Drisler	3,600	Librarian	900
" McCulloh	3,600	Clerk of Trustees	400
" Lieber	3,600	Treasurer	2,500
" Peck	3,600	Chaplain	300
" Nairne	3,600	Organist	200
" Joy	2,900	Janitor	700
" Joy's servant	200	Assistant Janitor	300

SALARIES.

1864, Jan. 11. In 1864, January 11, it was resolved that from the fifteenth of the February following the salaries of the officers should be as follows:

President, with use of his house	$3,500	Professor of chemistry, with house allowed him	$3,300
President's clerk	500	Professor of chemistry, for his servant	200
Jay professor of greek, including $1,000 for house-rent	4,000	Gebhard professor of german	1,800
Professor of latin, including $1,000 for house-rent	4,000	Professor of evidences of religion	1,000
Professor of history, including $1,000 for house-rent	4,000	Professor of higher mathematics	2,000
Professor of mathematics, including $1,000 for house-rent	4,000	Adjunct professor of mathematics	1,500
		Librarian	1,000
Professor of moral and intellectual philosophy, including $1,000 for house-rent	4,000	Clerk of board of trustees	500
		Treasurer	3,000
		Chaplain	200
		Organist	200
Professor of physics, including $1,000 for house-rent	4,000	Janitor, with his house	800
		Assistant janitor	300

1864, Feb. 1. On February 1st of same year, resolved that the salary of the adjunct professor of mathematics be made two thousand dollars, to date from February 15; and that the increase of salaries adopted January 11 date from November 15, 1863.

1864, June 6. *Resolved*, That the amounts reduced from the salaries of the president and professors, and the officers of the board and the college, be restored from the time of reduction, except in the case of professor McVickar, the reduction of whose salary was intended to be permanent.

1865, June 6. *Resolved*, That the salary of professor Lieber, in the faculty of law, be continued at the rate of four thousand dollars a year, until otherwise ordered by this board.

1865, June 19. *Resolved*, That the sum of one thousand dollars be paid to the president and each of the professors at full salary; and a proportionate sum to each of the other professors and tutors of the faculty of arts, and to the treasurer and clerk.

1865, Nov. 6. It was ordered that the salary of professor Lieber be paid out of the general funds of the college, and not from the fees received from the law students.

1865, July 6. A committee, consisting of Messrs. Jones, Strong, Dix, Ogden, and Rutherfurd, was appointed to consider the whole subject of salaries.

1866, Feb. 5. The committee made an elaborate report, concluding with resolutions, which, after modification, were adopted, as follows :

1866, Feb. 5. 1*st. Resolved,* That the salaries and compensation of the president, and of the several professors named in this resolution, and of the president's clerks, be established at the rates herein respectively mentioned, to be computed from the fifteenth day of November last past, to continue during the pleasure of the trustees, and to be in lieu and stead of all salary and compensation heretofore allowed to them, viz. :

President Barnard five thousand dollars per annum, together with the use and occupancy of the president's house, estimated at the annual rent or value of ten hundred dollars.

Professor Anthon four thousand dollars per annum.
Professor Drisler four thousand dollars per annum.
Professor Peck four thousand dollars per annum.
Professor Nairne four thousand dollars per annum.
Professor Rood four thousand dollars per annum.
Professor Joy four thousand dollars per annum, that is to say three thousand dollars in money, and the use and occupancy of the house in which he now resides, estimated at the annual rent or value of one thousand dollars.

Professor Schmidt eighteen hundred dollars per annum, without considering the amount paid to him from the Gebhard endowment.

Professor Van Amringe three thousand dollars per annum.

Professor Chandler one thousand dollars per annum as

dean of the school of mines, and in addition his salary as professor.

The president's clerk one thousand dollars per annum.
The chaplain, three hundred and fifty dollars.
The organist, two hundred and fifty dollars.

2d. *Resolved*, That the wages of the assistant janitor and of the janitor of the school of mines, severally, be established at the rate of fifty dollars per month, and that of the janitor of the law school at forty-five dollars per month, to be computed from the first day of October last, as recommended by the committee on the law school, such rates of wages to take effect and to be computed from the first day of January last past, and to be continued during the pleasure of the trustees.

3d. *Resolved*, That the salary and compensation of the several professors and employes of the college, other than those especially named in the two foregoing resolutions, is hereby declared to be continued during the pleasure of the trustees, at the rates mentioned in the statement furnished by the treasurer.

4th. *Resolved*, That a grant in the nature of a temporary increase of salary and compensation of twenty-five per cent. upon the salaries as heretofore paid from the fifteenth of August to the fifteenth of November, and upon the amount of their respective annual salaries and compensation as established or declared by the preceding resolutions, be made to each of the professors, officers, and tutors following, viz.: To the president, to professors Anthon, Drisler, Peck, Nairne, Rood, Joy, Schmidt, and Van Amringe; to the treasurer, the clerk, the chaplain, the organist, the janitor, and to the tutors of greek and latin, and of english literature and philosophy; that such last-mentioned grant be computed from the fifteenth of November last past; be payable quarterly or otherwise, as the salaries of the several parties entitled thereto are paid; and be continued for two years from such last-mentioned date, if the person to whom the same is granted as above, continue thus long in his present employment, and in the discharge of the duties thereof, as the same are or may be from time to time established by the trustees.

5th. *Resolved,* That when the trustees shall decide that instruction in the french and german languages shall be given in the school of mines, and shall appoint instructors or tutors, or both, of such languages, their salaries shall be at the rate of five hundred dollars per annum, each.

1867, Feb. 4. *Resolved,* That the salaries of the assistant in assaying, in the school of mines, and that of the assistant in charge of the laboratory for special students, be raised from five hundred to one thousand dollars.

1867, May 6. *Resolved,* That after the present academic year, the salaries of the registrar and assistants of the school of mines be paid in six equal instalments on the 15th of November, the 2d of January, the 15th of February, the 1st of April, the 15th of May, and the 1st of June of each year.

1868, Jan. 6. *Resolved,* That a grant in the nature of a temporary increase of salary and compensation of fifty per cent. upon the salaries as established by the resolution of this board of February 5, 1866, be made to each of the professors, officers, and tutors following, viz.: To the president, professors Drisler, Peck, Nairne, Rood, Joy, Schmidt, and Van Amringe; to the treasurer, the clerk, the chaplain, the organist, the janitor, and to the tutors of greek and latin, and of english literature and philosophy; that such last-mentioned grant be computed from the fifteenth day of November last past; be payable quarterly or otherwise, as the salaries of the several parties entitled thereto are paid; and be continued for one year from such last-mentioned date, if the person to whom the same is granted as above continue thus long in his present employment, and in the discharge of the duties thereof, as the same are or may be from time to time established by the trustees.

Resolved, That the salaries of professors Egleston, Vinton, Chandler, and Newberry be four thousand dollars per annum during the pleasure of the board; and that a grant in the nature of a temporary increase of salary, of twenty-five per cent. upon said salary, be made to each of said professors for one year, from the 15th day of November, 1867, if the said persons shall continue thus long in their present employments and in the discharge of the duties thereof, as the same are or may be from time to time established by the board of trustees, and that the allowance heretofore granted to Dr. Chandler as dean, be continued in addition to the salary and temporary increase thereof above mentioned; and that this resolution take effect from the fifteenth day of November, 1867.

1868, April 6. *Resolved*, That the treasurer be authorized to pay the salary of the president's secretary in monthly instalments.

SEAL.

1755, June 3. The governors of King's college adopted a device for a seal (prepared, it is said, by president Johnson) and ordered it to be engraved.

1784, May 4. The "regents of the university," who succeeded the governors of King's college, directed the preparation of a new seal; and such a seal seems to have been in use; but its device is not recorded.

1787, May 18. A committee (previously appointed by the trustees of Columbia college) reported still another device, which was approved and ordered to be engraved.

1788, March 28. By the following resolution, the trustees set aside the newly proposed seal, and readopted with a suitable modification the original device:

Resolved, That the former seal of the corporation of King's college be continued as the seal of this corporation without alteration, except that the following be the exergue, "COLLEGII COLUMBIÆ NOVI EBORACI SIGILLUM."

1865, June 19. *Resolved,* That the president and treasurer be authorized to cause the seal of the college to be engraved and transferred to a steel roller die for application to the diploma plates of the college, the school of law, and the school of mines, and to other official documents to which it may properly be applied; and that the treasurer be authorized to pay the expense thereof, not to exceed three hundred dollars.

SCHOLARSHIPS, FREE.

1827, Feb. 12. It was ordered that every school which should conform to a plan of preparatory instruction prescribed by the board of the college, and which should submit to visitation and examination by said board, should be entitled to send annually one scholar to the college free of all charge for tuition throughout the whole college course: provided said school should send also at the same time four other scholars duly qualified who should pay their fees.

1827, Dec. 3. The foregoing provision was reaffirmed, but the condition in regard to visitation, &c., was omitted.

1830, May 4. Four free scholarships were established, to be filled by scholars of the grammar school of distinguished promise, in indigent circumstances.

1851, Dec. 1. *Resolved,* That the nomination of two scholarships, conferred on the Clinton Hall association, by the statute of January, 1830, be and is hereby revoked, reserving the rights of one actual nominee to a completion of his course.

Resolved, That the two scholarships assigned by the same statute to the New York High school, which have lapsed, be revived, and that these, with the two heretofore held on the nomination of the Clinton Hall association, be assigned to the Free academy, on the nomination of the principal and professors thereof. Such nomination to be confined to the students of the academy, and that one scholar be annually named.

1853, Feb. 7. In 1853 it was resolved to receive one scholar on the plan proposed in the report of the secretary of state, whenever the legislature shall have given its sanction thereto, and shall provide means for carrying out the design; also, that any compensation allowed by the legislature to the college for such pupils shall be paid to said pupils to be applied to defraying the expense of books and boarding.

BEQUEST OF WM. B. MOFFAT, M. D.

1863, Oct. 5. The treasurer having informed this board that he had received from the executor of the late Wm. B. Moffat, M.D., the sum of two thousand dollars, bequeathed by the latter in the following clause of his will: "I give and bequeath unto Columbia college, in the city of New York, wherein I received my instruction, two thousand dollars for the purpose of one or more scholarships for the education of one or more students;" and also that the widow of Dr. Moffat has now in her possession and ready for delivery to the college, a copy of the "Biographie Universelle," which he purchased in his lifetime, and intended to present to this institution, but was prevented from so doing by accident. Thereupon—

Resolved, That the board desires to express its sense of the liberality of the late Dr. Moffat in making these gifts, and that his executor be informed that the above-mentioned payment will constitute a foundation for two free scholarships, which will be named the "Moffat scholarships," and the nomination to which will belong to the personal representatives of Dr. Moffat or their assigns.

SMITHSONIAN INSTITUTION, AGREEMENT WITH.

1865, Dec. 18. A letter from professor Henry, secretary of the Smithsonian institution, Washington, having been received by professor Egleston, of the school of mines, containing the following proposed terms of agreement:

"1. The duplicate and unassorted specimens of minerals now in the possession of the Smithsonian institution, or to be received hereafter, to be transmitted free of expense to the school of mines, Columbia college, to be taken charge of by you, and kept separate from the other collections of the college, and properly labelled.

"2. You to select the best of the specimens for the cabinet of the Smithsonian institution, as far as they may be required for that purpose.

"3. Duplicate specimens to be exchanged under your direction, for such minerals as may be needed to complete the Smithsonian collection.

"4. Series of greater or less extent, or single specimens, to be presented to first-class public collections of minerals in the name of the Smithsonian institution, and with its authority, as far as they may be required for that purpose.

"5. The best series of duplicate specimens to be retained by you for the use of Columbia college.

"6. The collections of specimens for the institution to be returned duly labelled and ready to be placed in the gallery of mineralogy."

Resolved, That this board consent to the agreement proposed to be entered into between the Smithsonian institution and Columbia college, as stated in the letter from professor Henry to professor Egleston.

1865, Dec. 18. *Resolved,* That professor Egleston be authorized to visit Washington with a view to the carrying out of this arrangement, and that the treasurer refund the necessary expenses of his visit.

1866, Nov. 5. *Resolved,* That a sum not exceeding fifty dollars be appropriated for the purpose of defraying any necessary expenses which may be incurred in carrying out the provisions of the former resolutions of this board in regard to the examination and classification of minerals from the Smithsonian institution.

1868, March 2. *Resolved,* That hereafter, the sum of fifty dollars be annually appropriated from the sum reserved for contingencies in the school of mines, to be applied to defray the expenses necessary for conducting the classification and selection of the Smithsonian minerals, as heretofore authorized by the trustees; this resolution to take effect from and after the first of October next.

1868, May 4. The foregoing resolution was reconsidered and amended so as to take effect October 1, 1867, and readopted as amended.

SOCIETIES, COLLEGE.

1860, May 7. *Resolved,* That the sum of two hundred dollars be appropriated to be expended under the direction of the president for procuring accommodations for each of the societies for the next academic year, provided that the property and libraries of the societies shall not be removed from the college.

1862, June 22. *Resolved,* That the appropriation made on May 7, 1860, for procuring accommodations for each of the college societies shall, until further order of this board, be considered to authorize the treasurer to pay the actual expense of procuring such accommodations, in each academic year, not to exceed for either society the sum of two hundred dollars for any year; provided, that the bill for such expense shall be approved by the president.

1866, Nov. 26. *Resolved,* That the Philolexian and Peithologian societies have leave to deposit their libraries in a room on the north-easterly corner of the second story of the college building, subject to such regulations as the president may appoint, and during the pleasure of the board.

SECRET SOCIETIES.

1860, Feb. 6. *Resolved,* That the president of the college be requested, by correspondence with the presidents of other colleges, and by such other means as he may deem expedient, to inquire and report to this board whether any, and if any what, measures are proper and necessary for the suppression of secret societies of the students of the college.

The result of this inquiry does not appear in the minutes.

SPORTS AND GAMES.

1857, Oct. 12. A petition of the students for inclosing a portion of the botanic garden property as a playground was referred to the standing committee with power.

1867, April 1. *Resolved,* That a sum not exceeding two hundred dollars be appropriated to be used under the direction of the acting president, to provide bats and other necessary instruments and appliances for the sports and exercises of the students in the open air.

1868, May 1. An additional appropriation of one hundred dollars was made at this date in further provision for the objects specified in the foregoing resolution.

STANDING COMMITTEE.

1824, Feb. 2. It was resolved that a committee, to consist of five members, to be styled the "standing committee," shall be appointed by the trustees, from their own body, whose duty it shall be to confer from time to time with the treasurer about the management and disposition of the funds and property of the college, to examine and audit the treasurer's accounts, and to report upon the same and the state of the college revenues and property at least once in every year, and whose further duty it shall be to visit the college frequently for the purpose of inquiring into its situation, and particularly of ascertaining whether the statutes, ordinances, and regulations are duly observed and carried into effect; to report to the board the names of such persons as they may deem entitled to honorary degrees, and generally to act upon all such matters as may from time to time be referred to them by the trustees.

Resolved, That the said committee shall in the first instance be appointed by ballot, and that one member of the said committee shall retire therefrom at the end of each six months, at the expiration of which times, respectively, the board shall appoint a trustee to fill the vacancy which shall then occur, and so from time to time thereafter, at the end of each six months, a trustee shall be appointed to supply the vacancy which shall take place, so that each trustee who shall hereafter be appointed on the said committee, shall continue to act for the period of two years and a half.

1827, March 5. *Resolved*, That the standing committee have power to give the consent of this corporation to the transfer of leases: and that in all cases in which the consent of this corporation has been or shall be given for the assignment of any leases, it shall be lawful for the clerk to sign and to affix the corporate seal to a certificate of such consent, to be prepared and signed by the treasurer.

1851, Jan. 6. *Resolved*, That the minutes of the standing committee hereafter be read at the stated meetings.

1855, Feb. 5. It was resolved that the standing committee shall be elected by ballot, and when the time of a member is about to expire, that the clerk be requested to state the fact to the trustees at a stated meeting preceding that at which the election to fill the vacancy shall take place.

1859, Feb. 7. *Resolved*, That the standing committee have power to audit and authorize the payment of all bills for ordinary supplies for the college after the same shall have been approved by the president, and also from time to time to direct such repairs to be made as they shall deem necessary, provided that the cost of any repairs so directed to be made between any two stated meetings of this board, shall not exceed two hundred dollars.

1859, Nov. 7. *Resolved*, That the standing committee be authorized to direct the sale of all or any part of the stone excavated from the upper estate of the college, and now upon the lots.

1859, Dec. 5. *Resolved*, That the standing committee be empowered to make application to the legislature for a law empowering the trustees of the college to acquire and hold lands within the block on which the college stands, between Forty-ninth and Fiftieth streets, the Fourth avenue and a line which would be the middle line of Madison avenue if extended; and that the clerk have power to affix the seal to any application for that purpose; and that the committee have power to purchase land within such limit.

1862, April 7. *Resolved*, That the standing committee inquire into the propriety and expediency of petitioning the corporation to direct the fencing of the lots opposite to the college grounds on Forty-ninth street, between the Fourth and Fifth avenues; and should they deem it proper and expedient, that they be empowered to present such petition.

1862, May 19. *Resolved*, That in all cases of arrears of rent now due upon college leases, the standing committee have power to direct the commencement and prosecution in the name of this corporation, of such suits and proceedings as may be deemed advisable for the recovery of such rent, or to obtain possession of the leasehold premises, or both; and also, in cases in which it may appear that it is for the interest of the college, owing to the embarrassments or doubtful responsibility of the tenants, to accept composition of the amount due for such rent, and thereupon to accept surrenders of the leases, and direct the execution on tho part of the college of releases of all claims and demands by reason of the covenant in such leases contained.

1863, Oct. 5. A resolution was adopted in language almost identical with the foregoing, and extending the provisions to arrears for taxes and assessments as well as to those for rents.

1862, May 19. *Resolved,* That the consents for the transfers of leases granted under the authority heretofore conferred on the standing committee be confirmed.

Resolved, That the standing committee have power to grant consents to the transfers of leases by way of mortgage or absolute assignment, and the clerk to affix the corporate seal of the college to such consents.

On motion of the treasurer—

Resolved, That the treasurer be authorized to agree, under the direction of the standing committee, for the extension of the time of payment of such bonds of the college as are due; or under the like direction to substitute new bonds for them for the same amount: the old and new bonds to be made payable at such time as to the committee shall seem expedient.

1864, Jan. 11. No payments on account of appropriations for departments of instruction shall be made by the treasurer until the bills therefor shall have been audited by the standing committee

1864, Feb. 1. *Resolved,* That the standing committee have power, should it seem to them expedient, from time to time to discontinue the employment of any agent, and to appoint another to render assistance under their direction in effecting leases of the property of the upper estates; and also power to allow such compensation to the agent as the interest of the college may seem to require.

1864, April 4. The standing committee was invested with power to make agreements with tenants for the erection of party walls; and the clerk was empowered to affix the seal of the college to all papers drawn in pursuance of the above authority.

1864, May 2. *Resolved*, That the committee have power to make with lessees of lots in the upper estate such modifications of the covenants and conditions in their leases in respect to the time for building, and upon such terms, as shall to the committee appear expedient; provided that the time for such building shall not be extended for more than three years from the first day of May instant; and that the clerk affix the seal of the corporation to all instruments which may be authorized by the standing committee under this resolution.

1864, May 18. On May 18, 1864, it was resolved, that the standing committee have power to place in the ante-room leading to the library, the tablet inscribed to the memory of John Sym, formerly in the library of the old college.

1867, Feb. 4. *Resolved*, That the treasurer be authorized to invest in the name of this corporation, under the direction of the standing committee, five thousand dollars, or about that amount, of the funds which will be in his hands on the fifteenth day of February instant, in stocks of the United States, or of the state of New York, or of the city of New York; and also from time to time, until the end of the present financial year, to invest in like manner, and under the like direction, any sum that in the judgment of the committee will probably not be required to meet the expenditures of the year.

Resolved, also, That the treasurer have power, under the like direction, if it seem to the standing committee necessary, to convert into money the investments made under the last preceding resolution, and to assign any securities that may be held for the same; and that the clerk affix the corporate seal to any instruments necessary in the premises.

1867, April 1. The recommendation of the standing committee that the trustees should give them authority to waive forfeitures of leases for non-compliance with the covenant for building, and to extend the time for such purpose in such cases as they may deem expedient and for the interest of the college, and to direct the execution of all necessary instruments under the corporate seal for effecting such waiver or extension, was approved; and the requisite authority was granted.

1867, Nov. 4. *Resolved,* That the standing committee have power in relation to that part of the land of the college, in the block of ground between 49th and 50th streets, and the Fifth and Sixth avenues, which lies west of a line drawn parallel to the Fifth avenue, at a distance of three hundred and fifty feet therefrom, to make such terms for leasing the same as they shall deem reasonable.

1867, Dec. 2. *Resolved,* That in all cases in which rents for one or more years shall be in arrear, the standing committee be authorized to direct such measures to be taken as may be deemed expedient to enforce the rights of the college.

Resolved, also, That in every such case of rents in arrear for one year or more, the standing committee, if they shall deem it for the interest of the college so to do, may authorize the acceptance of a surrender of the existing lease, and make an agreement for the payment or composition of the amount due upon the covenants in the lease.

1867, Dec. 18. *Resolved,* That the standing committee inquire whether any repairs or constructions are required in or about the president's house, with power to make such as in their judgment may be needed.

TRANSFER OF STUDENTS FROM CLASS TO CLASS.

1842, Dec. 5. *Resolved,* That whenever application is made to advance a student from a lower to a higher class otherwise than according to the course contemplated by the statutes of the college, the president shall report to the board of trustees a statement of all the circumstances on which the application is founded. If the board of trustees shall thereupon consent, the student is to be publicly examined by the faculty, and, if found qualified, may be admitted to the higher class.

TREASURER.

1841, Dec. 13. *Resolved,* That the treasurer be authorized to institute any legal steps he may deem necessary to recover any rent that now is or may be due and in arrears to the college, and that the clerk be authorized to affix the seal of the college to any warrant which the treasurer may require in execution of the authority hereby conferred.

1842, Jan. 3. *Resolved,* That the college fiscal year shall hereafter terminate on the Saturday next preceding the last Wednesday in September in each year.

1842, Jan. 6. On January 6th of the same year it was resolved that all payments of tuition fees should be made directly to the treasurer.

1850, Jan. 7. *Resolved,* That the treasurer be authorized in all cases of non-payment of rent now due or to become due to the college, to institute such proceedings as may be authorized by the leases or agreements pertaining thereto, and in such cases that the clerk affix the seal of the college.

TRUSTEES.

1851, April 7. *Resolved,* That whenever the treasurer shall think proper, under the resolution of this board passed January 7, 1850, to institute any suit or proceedings in case of non-payment of rent due or to become due to the college, he shall be authorized to appoint one or more attorneys to commence in the name of the college any action or proceedings authorized by that resolution, and that the clerk be authorized to affix the seal of the college to all or any such appointments.

1863, Oct. 5. *Resolved,* That Gouverneur M. Ogden, the treasurer of the corporation, be authorized to receive from time to time, as it shall accrue, the interest on any stock, bonds, or evidences of indebtedness of the United States of America, standing in the name of the corporation, and to give all proper receipts and acquittances for the same.

TRUSTEES.

1835, April 6. At a stated meeting of this date it was ordered—

That whenever any trustee shall have absented himself from five successive meetings of the board, it shall be the duty of the clerk to give a written notice to such trustee that by the provisions of the charter his seat is liable to be vacated, and that the clerk at the next meeting of the board report the fact of such absence and notice.

1843, Oct. 2. By resolution of October 2, 1843, it was ordered that copies of the new statutes with intermediate blank leaves be kept upon the table, and that alterations from time to time made in the statutes be entered and noted in those copies.

1851, Feb. 3. It was ordered that the hour of meeting hereafter should be two o'clock, P. M.

1835, Feb. 4. The day, hour, and place of meeting of the trustees have been often changed. Since Feb. 4, 1835, the day

1859, June 6. has been the first Monday in the month; since June 6, 1859, the place has been the law school; and since the
1851, Feb. 3. date of the order above cited, the hour has been two o'clock in the afternoon. In later years the stated meetings of one or more of the summer months have been omitted, by special resolution to that effect, or by adjournment from June or July to September or October.

RULES OF ORDER.

1860, Nov. 3. The following rules of order, to be observed at the meetings of the trustees, were adopted Nov. 3, 1860:

First.—Upon an appearance of a quorum, the chairman of the board shall call it to order; should he be absent, a chairman *pro tempore* shall be appointed. If a quorum shall not appear within half an hour from the time appointed for meeting, the members present shall adjourn; and they may adjourn to a stated time, of which notice shall be given as of a stated meeting.

Second.—The order of business, except as hereinafter provided, shall be as follows:

1. The roll shall be called by the clerk.
2. The minutes of the preceding meeting shall be read and passed upon.
3. The minutes of the standing committee shall be read.
4. The president shall read the minutes of the board of the college.
5. The recommendations of the standing committee, and other matters reported by them, shall be considered
6. Motions by the treasurer.
7. Communications from the president.*

---

* Added by an amendment of January 2, 1866.

8. Matters appearing in the minutes of the board of the college which shall require the action of the trustees.

9. Special orders.

10. The reports of committees shall be received and considered.

11. The clerk shall announce the vacancies that may exist in any of the standing committees, or that should be filled therein.

12. Nominations for vacancies that may exist in the body of trustees.

13. Elections to fill such vacancies.

14. Elections to fill vacancies in the office of chairman, treasurer, or clerk of the board; or in any of the standing committees. The vote to fill such vacancies shall be by ballot.

15. Motions not arising from any of the subjects heretofore mentioned.

16. Communications to the trustees shall be received and disposed of.

17. Miscellaneous business.

Third.—Any member wishing to submit a motion, or to make any remarks, shall rise and address the chair. If more than one claims the floor, the chairman shall award it to the one who rose first.

Fourth.—No motion shall be received unless the same be submitted in writing; nor shall it be considered until it be seconded. It shall not be necessary to enter upon the minutes that it was seconded; the record of its having been put shall be evidence of such seconding. Motions, however, to lay on the table, to postpone, either indefinitely or to a day certain, to commit or to adjourn, need not be in writing.

Fifth.—When a question is before the board, no motion

shall be received, except a motion to lay on the table, to postpone indefinitely, to postpone to a certain time, to commit, or to amend; which motions shall have precedence in the order named.

Sixth.—All amendments shall be considered in the order in which they are received. When a proposed amendment is under consideration, a motion to amend the same may be made; no further amendment to such second amendment shall be in order. But when an amendment to an amendment is under consideration, a substitute for the whole matter may be received. No proposition on a subject different from that under consideration shall be received under color of a substitute.

Seventh.—A motion to lay on the table, or for indefinite postponement, shall be decided without debate.

Eighth.—A motion to adjourn shall always be in order when no member is speaking, and shall be decided without debate.

Ninth.—The mover may withdraw a motion or resolution at any time before a vote shall have been taken upon it, or before amendment, in which case it shall not be entered upon the minutes.

Tenth.—If a question under debate contain several distinct propositions, the same shall be divided at the request of any member, and a vote taken separately.

Eleventh.—No member may speak more than twice on the same question without leave of the board, nor more than once until every member wishing to speak shall have had an opportunity of so doing.

Twelfth.—Every member present shall vote whenever a question is put, unless excused by the board.

Thirteenth.—A question being decided shall not be reconsidered, unless the motion to reconsider be made at or before the stated meeting next after such decision; nor unless the motion for that purpose be made by one of the majority on the first decision. No question shall be reconsidered more than once.

Fourteenth.—All special committees shall be appointed by the chairman, unless otherwise ordered.

Fifteenth.—The reports of all committees shall be in writing, and shall be received, of course, without motion for acceptance. They shall be entered upon the minutes unless otherwise ordered. If recommending or requiring any action or expression of opinion by the board, they shall be accompanied by a resolution or resolutions.

Sixteenth.—When a member is called to order by the chairman, or by another member, he shall immediately sit down, unless permitted to explain. All questions of order shall be determined by the chairman—but any member may appeal from the decision of the chair; and on such appeal, no member shall speak more than once without leave of the board.

Seventeenth.—The prescribed order of business shall not be departed from, nor shall any rule of order be suspended, except by unanimous consent; nor shall any rule be changed or rescinded, unless notice of a motion to that effect be given at a previous stated meeting, which notice shall be entered upon the minutes.

Eighteenth.—At special meetings it shall not be necessary to read the minutes of the standing committee, or of the board of the college.

1860, Dec. 3. *Resolved,* That the clerk be required to collect and report to this board the permanent rules and resolutions now in force, and that he be empowered to employ such assistance as he may deem necessary.

1861, Feb. 4. *Resolved,* That it be referred to a special committee of three persons to inquire into the practice of holding stated and special meetings, and the authority for holding the same, and that they report thereon.

Mr. Allen, Mr. Betts, and Mr. Strong were appointed the committee.

No report of this committee appears in the minutes of the board.*

---

* The following resolutions embrace probably the information which it was the object of this proceeding to elicit:

1796, April 19. *Resolved,* That in future the board assemble for the purpose of conferring degrees on the second Tuesday in April in every year.

1810, May 7. *Resolved,* That, besides the annual meeting previous to commencement, the board will in future regularly meet on the first Mondays in January, March, May, July, September, and November, at eleven o'clock in the forenoon of each of the days aforesaid.

1816, Sept. 2. *Resolved,* That the meetings of the board, after the present month, be held on the first Thursday of every month, in the college, at four o'clock in the afternoon.

This last resolution established the rule that stated meetings should be held monthly; but the board have, by resolution, sometimes omitted one or more successive stated meetings, especially during the summer months; and the day of the week, and the week in the month, in which the meetings should be held, have been subject to frequent changes. On 1817, Jan. 2. the second of January, 1817, the day was changed from the first Thursday to the first Monday; and this day has generally prevailed, though it has sometimes temporarily given place to Tuesday or Wednesday. In 1827, March 6. 1827, the third Monday of the month was substituted for the first. This, 1828, Feb. 4. 1833, March 4. in 1828, was changed to the first Tuesday; and again in 1833 to the first 1835, Feb. 4. Wednesday; and afterwards, in 1835, to the first Monday once more. In 1859, Feb. 7. 1859, Mar. 8. 1859, a resolution was adopted to return to the third Monday; but at the next meeting of the board this resolution was reconsidered and lost.

The resolution of April 19, 1796, is the earliest standing order on the subject of meeting which appears in the minutes. While the "regents of the university" had charge of the college, their meetings were frequent but irregular; and the time of each succeeding meeting was fixed at the meeting next preceding. This practice was continued by the trustees of Columbia college, appointed in 1787, who met for the first time on the eighth day of May in that year. This body seems not to have been, in the beginning at least, remarkably zealous. After holding three meetings, and succeeding in electing a president, they failed on four successive at-

1867, Dec. 18. *Resolved,* That the entry on the minutes of the trustees of the report to the regents be dispensed with, and that a copy be preserved when it shall be printed in the annual report of the regents.

TUTORSHIPS.

1858, March 8. *Resolved,* That it be referred to a committee to inquire and report as to the expediency of appointing one or more tutors in the college, and for what terms, at what compensation, and with what power.

1859, Jan. 3. This committee appears not to have reported; but on the 3d of January, 1859, a communication was received from the faculty recommending the appointment of three tutors: one in the mathematical and one in the classical

---

tempts in as many weeks, to secure a quorum for business, and finally adjourned *sine die.* Five months later they reassembled "in pursuance of public notification." This notification was probably given by the clerk, under the provision of the charter which authorizes any five of the governors, "by writing and under their hands," to direct that officer to advertise such a meeting "in one or more of the public newspapers." To adjourn *sine die* became subsequently not an unfrequent thing; and it was also not unusual to adjourn *die in diem* until a quorum could be obtained. Fifteen members were required, under the royal charter, to constitute a quorum; the act of April 13, 1787, revising the charter, reduced this number to thirteen, and the amended charter of March 23, 1810, fixed the number required for a quorum at eleven.

The original charter "ordains and directs" that the governors of the college shall "yearly and every year hereafter, forever," meet on the second Tuesday of May; leaving them free to meet at such other times as they may please. Until the revolution, this provision was duly observed. The regents of the university, however, paid no regard to it; and the trustees of Columbia college, though the act which gave them authority gave them also the royal charter, with only a change of style, as their organic law, respected it as little. By what may have been an accident, their first meeting, held May 8, 1787, fell upon the second Tuesday of May. A similar accident happened on Tuesday, May 14, 1805, and on Tuesday, May 9, 1865; but with these exceptions the trustees of Columbia college have never met on the day of the year appointed by the charter for their anniversary meeting. The amended charter, which was passed by the legislature on the 23d of March, 1810, omits to prescribe the day for the anniversary meeting, so that the injunction of the royal charter may be considered as having been at that time virtually abrogated.

department, with one tutor at large; which was referred to the committee known as the committee of inquiry.

1859, April 4. This committee reported in favor of appointing only one tutor, viz., a tutor of mathematics; and Emory McClintock, then a member of the senior class, was immediately appointed tutor of mathematics, the degree of bachelor of arts being conferred on him at the same time.

The resolution under which Mr. McClintock was appointed established a tutorship in the department of mathematics at eight hundred dollars per year, to be held during the pleasure of the board. The tutor was to give to the students instruction, subject to the professor of mathematics; and at such times as should be fixed in the scheme of attendance. Said tutor to have a seat at the board of the college when the conduct or proficiency of students under his charge should be in question; but on no other occasion; and to have no vote.

1860, Nov. 5. By resolution of November 5, 1860, there were ordered to be appointed three tutors; one in greek, one in latin, and a second tutor in mathematics; each to receive compensation at the rate of ———— hundred dollars per year; the appointments to date from the commencement of the next term; nominations for such appointments to be made at the next stated meeting of the board.

1861, June 24. No such nominations were, however, made at the following, or at any subsequent meeting; and on June 24, 1861, the action of the board in regard to this subject was by resolution indefinitely postponed.

1864, April 11. A tutorship in latin and greek was created by the appointment of Mr. Duane Shuler Everson.

1865, Sept. 25. A tutorship of english literature was created by the appointment of Mr. Eugene Lawrence.

ELOCUTION, INSTRUCTION IN.

1860, Nov. 5. The board of the college having recommended that the services of a competent teacher of elocution be provided, it was—

Resolved, That the subject be referred to a special committee, to report at the next stated meeting of the board.

1860, Dec. 3. *Resolved*, That the president be authorized to make arrangements for instruction in elocution so as not to interfere with the regular course of study; merit-marks to be given in this department as well as in the others.

UNIVERSITY CONVOCATION.

1863, May 4. A communication from the chancellor of the regents of the university to the chairman of this board, accompanied by a circular, and a correspondence between the chancellor, Mr. Pruyn, and President King, proposing an annual meeting of officers of colleges and academies for the purpose of discussing the subject of education, were on May 4, 1863, presented by the chairman of the board. The papers were referred to the faculty, and they were authorized to send delegates from their number to the proposed meeting at Albany, should they deem it expedient to do so.

VISITATION OF THE COLLEGE.

1857, June 5. *Resolved*, That there shall be a visiting committee, to consist of three trustees, who shall meet once in each fortnight at the college, during recitation hours, through the year. It shall be the duty of the committee to visit the several rooms and apartments of the building, the grounds, etc., and inquire into their condition, to see whether the property of the college is attended to, and the laws carried out, and to inspect the minutes of the board of the college. A book, to be kept by them, shall show their attendance, proceedings, and observations in regard to the general manner in which the college is conducted. The president of the college shall be exempt from duty on this committee. He must, however, give notice to each trustee whose term is about to commence; and the chairman will announce the names of the trustees whose term will expire during the month, and of those who will respectively take their places.

WEIGHTS, MEASURES, AND COINS.

1864, April 4. *Resolved*, That in view of important international movements in progress for the purpose of establishing a uniform system of weights, measures, and coins for the use of the civilized world, it be referred to the president and faculty of the college to prepare and submit to this board a memorial to the congress of the United States in behalf of this college, expressing its sense of the importance of the measure in question.

1864, May 18. In accordance with this resolution the faculty of the college prepared and submitted, May 18, a memorial to congress, which was referred to a select committee. The committee reported it, with certain verbal corrections, on the sixth of June; whereupon it was—

1864, June 6. *Resolved*, That the memorial, as now reported, be engrossed and transmitted to the speaker of the house of representatives at Washington.

SUPPLEMENTARY.

The resolutions and abstracts of proceedings following were omitted in their proper order:

ACADEMIC DRESS.

The first mention of this subject which appears in the records of the college, is contained in a body of "laws, ordinances and orders," adopted by the governors of King's college on the 1st day of March, 1763, and "promulged in the college hall" on the day following. In this code it is enacted, under the head "of admission," that—

1763, March 1. "Each person admitted as above shall procure, within fourteen days of his entrance, a proper academical habit in which he shall always appear (unless he have leave of the president or tutors) under penalty of two shillings for the first offence (and so on in proportion) or adequate exercise."

The following resolution appears in the early minutes of the trustees of Columbia college:

1787, Dec. 3. *Resolved*, That it be recommended to the president and professors of the college to wear gowns.

ATTENDANCE AT PRAYERS.

1865, Nov. 6. A communication was received from Dr. S. Adler, asking that his son, who is a member of the sophomore class, and is destined for the Jewish ministry, may be excused from attendance on religious exercises in the chapel. Whereupon the following preamble and resolutions were adopted:

Whereas, The statutes and observances of the college are well known and are publicly announced, and whereas all students entering the college are bound to conform to such laws and observances; therefore—

Resolved, That the application of Dr. Adler be declined.

CHAIR OF GOV. CLINTON.

1828, July 1. Dr. Mathews informed the board that Mr. Charles Clinton, son of the late governor of this state, had presented to the college the chair in which his father was seated at the time of his death. Whereupon it was—

Resolved, That this board accept with grateful veneration for the memory of the late governor Clinton, an alumnus of this college, the chair in which he was seated at the time of his death, and which has been presented to the college by his son, Charles Clinton, Esq.

Resolved, That a committee be appointed to transmit a copy of this resolution to Mr. Clinton, and to report to the board as to the place in which the chair shall be deposited, and the occasions on which it shall be used, and that the committee cause a suitable plate and inscription to be placed upon the same. Bishop Hobart, Dr. Harris, and Col. Fish, were appointed the committee.

The plate and inscription provided for in this resolution were never prepared; and the chair itself had no place assigned to it until the year 1864. The chair was at that time in the room of the president, and had, perhaps, remained there for the thirty or forty years preceding, when the following resolution was adopted, and carried into execution:

1864, Dec. 5.   *Resolved*, That the chair presented to the college by Charles A. Clinton, Esq., formerly belonging to his father, DeWitt Clinton, and in which his father expired, be repaired; and that a plate containing a suitable inscription be placed thereon under the direction of the president; and further, that the chair be kept in the college library.

EXAMINATIONS.

1865, July 6.   *Resolved*, That it be referred to the president to confer with the faculty of arts upon the expediency of discontinuing the intermediate examination, and of increasing the strictness of that at the conclusion of the academic year; also, of establishing a special and stringent examination for honors; and to report to this board.

1865, Sept. 25.   The president reported unfavorably to the discontinuance of the intermediate examination; and favorably to the principle of instituting two orders of examinations; " of which the first shall be confined to authors read on subjects taught in the course of collegiate instruction, and to the limits of the actual course itself; while the second shall embrace a wider range, and be designed to measure the full extent of the student's attainments." The first to be compulsory upon all students; the second to apply only to volunteers. He submitted, however, that it would be premature to establish such a system of twofold examinations, until after a number of scholarships and fellowships of substantial value sufficient to stimulate emulation, should have been created.

FREE TUITION.

1812, Aug. 1.   *Resolved,* That the members of the board of the college be exempted from paying tuition money for the education of such of their children as may, from time to time, be students in the college.

The statutes further provide for free scholarships, as follows :

Two to each of the following bodies, viz.: Corporation of New York city; and of Brooklyn city; Mercantile Library Association; Mechanics' Institute; General Society of Mechanics and Tradesmen in New York city; American Institute; four to the Alumni Association of the college; one to the corporation of Jersey city, to each religious denomination in New York city, and to each school which may send four students who pay their fees.

PRIZE FELLOWSHIPS AND SCHOLARSHIPS.

1865, Oct. 9.   The following resolutions were presented by the president in the board of trustees, October 9, 1865, and read, ordered to be printed, and made the special order for November 6, 1865.

FELLOWSHIPS.

Resolved, by the board of trustees of Columbia college, That there shall be established in the college a fellowship, to be called the . . . . fellowship, of the annual value of . . . . . dollars, to be held by the successful competitor for the term of three years, and to be conferred under the conditions hereinafter provided, viz.:

Said fellowship shall be open for competition to such students of each graduating class as have been members of the college for the . . . preceding years, and as stand, in the reports of their final collegiate examination, in the first grade of scholarship, and have no grave censure for misconduct recorded against them upon the minutes of the faculty.

The examination for said fellowship shall commence on a day to be fixed by the board of the college, as early as may be convenient after the college examination, and shall embrace the subjects taught in the last two years of the collegiate course, and also the pure mathematics. These studies shall be classified under the two heads, *Literæ Humaniores* and *Disciplinæ Mathematicæ*. The range of the examination shall extend beyond the limits of the collegiate course. The student may select any books (at least . . . in number), on which to be examined in each department, from a list to be prepared and made public in advance, for the present, by the head of the department. These lists to be announced immediately for the present senior class; and, for future classes, at least two years in advance of the examination for the fellowship.

The examinations shall be in writing, and the competitors shall all be subjected to the same tests. The results shall be estimated according to a scale of values previously assigned to the question papers in each department of study; and the student whose performances shall receive under this regulation the highest number of marks, shall be entitled to the fellowship; provided such number does not fall below a fixed standard previously determined by the committee of examination as the minimum of excellence.

The examination shall be conducted by a committee of five; two, for the present, to be selected by the board of the college from their own number, and two by the board of trustees from their own number, the president of the college being the fifth member of the committee and the chairman. When there shall be a sufficient number of fellows, the examiners may be taken from the fellows of the college.

Each competitor shall adopt some motto, sentence, or word, with which he shall sign or endorse his examination papers, instead of employing his own name; and he shall inclose the same along with his name in a sealed envelope endorsed with the same word, sentence, or motto, which shall be handed to the chairman of the committee of examination.

The moneys which may become annually due under this resolution shall be paid in four equal instalments, on the . . . . . day of October, January, April, and June, in each year.

This resolution shall take effect immediately.

SCHOLARSHIPS.

Resolved, by the board of trustees of Columbia college, That there shall be established in the college three scholarships of the annual value of two hundred dollars each, to be called the . . . . scholarships, to be held by the successful competitors for the same, for the term of one year after each competition, and to be conferred under the conditions hereinafter provided, viz.:

The first of the aforesaid scholarships to be open for competition to such members of the freshman class, at the end of the freshman year, as have been members of the college for the entire collegiate year preceding, and as are embraced in the honor list of the year, and have no grave censure for misconduct recorded against them upon the minutes of the faculty. At the end of the sophomore year, this scholarship shall be again thrown open to competition, on the same terms as those hereinafter prescribed for the second scholarship above established.

The second scholarship shall be open for competition to any members of the sophomore class, at the end of the sophomore year, who have been members of the class for the two entire collegiate years preceding, whose names are in the superior honor list of their class, and who have no grave censure for misconduct recorded against them on the minutes of the faculty. At the end of the junior year, both this and the first scholarship above provided for shall be again open to competition, on the terms hereinafter prescribed for the third of the scholarships above established.

The third scholarship shall be open for competition to any members of the junior class who have been members of the class for the two preceding years, and who stand in the first class of honor in the record of college scholarship, and have no grave censure recorded against them in the minutes of the faculty.

The examinations for said scholarships shall commence on a day to be fixed by the board of the college, as early as may be after the close of the college examination, and shall embrace the subjects taught in college during the preceding portion of the collegiate course; but the range of examination shall extend beyond the limits of the course, and shall be determined in the same manner as is prescribed for the examinations for fellowships.

The examinations shall be conducted by the same committee who superintend the examinations for fellowships, and in all respects in accordance with the rules laid down for those examinations.

The payments which may become annually due under this resolution, to be made as follows, viz.: One hundred dollars to each scholar on the first Monday of October, which sum may be commuted for tuition, and the remainder in four equal instalments, to be paid on the days when the payments are made on account of fellowships.

This resolution shall take effect immediately.

1865, Dec. 4. The consideration of the foregoing resolutions was from time to time postponed; and on the fourth of December they were finally referred to the committee on the permanent financial policy of the college, who, in the ordinance reported by them February 5, 1866, and subsequently adopted November 26, 1866, made provision with a view to carrying them into effect when the resources of the college should allow.

REMOVAL OF THE COLLEGE.

1868, June 1. A committee was appointed to inquire and report as to the practicability of obtaining for the college buildings a more eligible site than that which they occupy at present; and as to the expediency in such case of taking measures with a view to the removal of the college from its present location at some future time.

REPAIRS.

1865, June 19. Authority was given to the standing committee to make such repairs on the houses of Dr. Torrey and professor Joy as they may deem necessary.

SEAL.

The early history of the college seal is briefly given on page 133. The following more detailed account may not be without interest.

1755, May 7. The first meeting of the governors of King's college was held on Wednesday, the seventh day of May, 1755. The business transacted on this occasion consisted of little more than the presentation and acceptance of the charter, and of the induction of the governors into office, each of whom took an oath, "to execute the trust reposed in him according to the best of his skill and understanding."

1755, May 13. The day fixed by the charter for the anniversary meeting, to be held "yearly, and every year hereafter forever," was the second Tuesday in May, which fell this year six days after the organization of the board. At this first stated meeting several committees were appointed, and among them one, of which Edward Holland, mayor of the city of New York, was chairman, "to prepare such devices and inscriptions as they shall think proper for the seal of this corporation," and also "to make a proper collection of prayers, and prepare a body of laws, rules, and regulations for the use and government of the college; and lay the same before this board with all convenient speed."

1755, June 3. This committee reported on the third day of June following, their report as to what concerns the seal, being in these words:

"*First.* That we are of opinion that the Device for a Seal produced to the Corporation, by Doctor Johnson, at the last meeting, and hereunto annexed, is a proper Device for a Seal for the College."

The board concurred in opinion with the committee, and adopted the device, of which the following is the description literally copied from the minutes:

"THE DEVICE OF THE COLLEGE SEAL.

"The College is represented by a Lady sitting in a Throne or Chair of State, with Severall Children at her knees to represent the Pupils, with I Peter, II, 1, 2, 7 v., under them to express the Temper with which they should apply Themselves to seek for True Wisdom. The words are, Wherefore laying aside all Malice and all Guile, and Hypocrisies and Envies and Evil Speakings, as New-born Babes desire the Sincere Milk of the Word that ye may grow thereby, &c. One of them She takes by the hand with her left hand expressing her benevolent design of Conducting them to true Wisdom and Virtue. To which purpose She holds open to them a Book in her right hand in which is [in] Greek Letters, ΛΌΓΙΑ ΖῶΝΤΑ, the living or lively Oracles, which is the Epithet that St. Stephen gives to the Holy Scriptures.—Acts 7 : 38. Out of her Mouth over her left Shoulder, goes a Label with these words in Hebrew Letters ORI-EL—God is my Light; alluding to Ps. 27: 1, expressing her Acknowledgment of God the Father of Lights, as the Fountain of all that Light both Natural and Revealed with which She proposes to inlighten or instruct her Children or Pupils;

whereof the Sun rising under the Label is the Emblem or Hieroglyphic, alluding to that expression Mal: IV. 2. The Sun of Righteousness arising with healing in his Wings. Over her head is Jehovah in a Glory, the Beams coming triangularly to a Point near her head, with these words round her for her Motto, IN LUMINE TUO VIDEBIMUS LUMEN—*In thy light shall we see light.*—Psal. 36 : 9. On the Edge round are engraved in Capitals, SIGILLUM COLLEGII REG. NOV. EBOR. IN AMERICA—*The Seal of King's College at New York in America.*"

The Board at the same time passed the following order :

"*Ordered*, That the said Committee cause a Seal to be forthwith made for this Corporation, to be cutt upon Silver, with such Devices and Inscriptions as aforesaid."

1784, May 1. In 1784, an act was passed by the legislature of the state of New York, entitled "an act for granting certain privileges to the college heretofore called King's college, for altering the name and charter thereof, and erecting a university within this state." This act created a body-corporate under the name and title of "the regents of the university," to whom were transferred the powers and duties previously confided to the governors of King's college.

1784, May 4. This body held its first meeting on the fourth of May, three days after the passage of the law, and one of its first acts was to appoint a committee "for the purpose of devising a seal for this corporation, which seal, when made, shall be lodged in the hands of the chancellor," &c., &c. Nothing appears in the minutes of the regents to show that this committee ever reported, or that the device prepared by them ever received the approval of the board ; but the corporate seal was occasionally ordered to be affixed to documents, from which we may infer that there was a seal recognized by the body as legitimate; and this could hardly have been the seal of King's college.

1787, May 8. At the first meeting of the trustees of Columbia college, held on Tuesday, May 8, 1787, the first business which received attention after organization, was the appointment of a committee, consisting of John H. Livingston, Samuel Bard, and Brockholst Livingston, to devise
1787, May 18. a seal. This committee, on the eighteenth of the same month, reported a device; which was approved and ordered to be engraved. The device, however, appears not to have given satisfaction; for, some ten months later, the resolution given on page 133 was introduced and passed, re-adopting the seal of King's college with a change of exergue as the seal of the new corporation.

The seal of the committee was nevertheless engraved as directed; for we find in the month of April following the order for the payment of the engraver:

1788, April 8. *Ordered,* That the treasurer pay to Peter R. Maverick one pound six shillings, being the amount of his account for making a silver seal and altering another.

It would be interesting to know what became of the rejected seal, and what was the device it bore. On neither point is curiosity likely to be gratified. As to the device, a space was left by the clerk in the minutes of the board for the description; but this space remains blank to this day.

TREASURER.

1865, May 9. *Ordered,* That the treasurer pay the annual water tax upon the president's house.

TRUSTEES.

1861, Feb. 25. *Resolved,* That under the direction of the treasurer the drawers of the table in the trustees' room be subdivided, and provided with keys, so that each trustee may have one.

1863, Feb. 2. *Resolved,* That the law committee be requested to take such measures as may be necessary to prevent the meetings of this board from being interrupted.

1867, Dec. 18. *Resolved,* That the warden of the law school be requested to cause the drawers of the tables in the room of the trustees to be cleared of the books and papers belonging to the students of the law school now in them, and also to cause said drawers and their locks to be put in good condition; and that said drawers be henceforth reserved for the exclusive use of members of the board of trustees; and that the committee on the law school be authorized to provide closets for the use of the students of the school.

Resolved, That a copy of the last preceding resolution be given to the warden of the law school, and to the chairman of the committee on the law school.

CORRECTIONS.

PAGE 5.—To the committee on the school of law should be added the name of SAMUEL BLATCHFORD, LL. D., immediately after that of THEODORE W. DWIGHT, LL. D.

PAGE 21.—After the word "resolutions," in line 21, insert the words, "which were adopted."

PAGE 28.—The imperfect marginal date should be "1839, June 3."

INDEX.

	PAGE
Absences of a trustee, five, work forfeiture of seat	145
" " " clerk to give notice of five successive	145

Academic department, appropriations for—*see* "Appropriations."
Academical dress...9, 155
Accommodations to be furnished for cloaks, books, etc..................... 23
Accumulating fund, provided for... 33
      "   " how to be applied... 35
      "   " managers of... 35
Advertising, appropriations for—*see* "Appropriations."
Agent for upper estates, to be employed by standing committee............. 141
Agreement with Smithsonian institute respecting minerals..............136, 137
      " to be made with tenants respecting party-walls................... 142
Allowance for house rent to professors.........................118, 128, 129, 130
      " to certain college officers.................................129, 131, 132
Alumni association, prize of.. 116
Alumni, governors, etc., of the college, catalogue of....................17, 18
Analytical geometry made an optional study................................. 64
Anatomy and physiology, course of, for senior class proposed............... 65
      "   "   " course of, elementary, to be given in law school.... 73
Ancient geography, required for admission.................................. 65
      "   " text-book in, president to report........................ 65
Ancient and modern literature, chair of, united with another............... 119
Anderson, Henry J., made emeritus professor................................ 124
Annual catalogue... 18
Anthon, professor, prize founded in honor of............................... 116
Apparatus, etc., room for in new college building.......................... 51
      " belonging to the college, catalogue of........................... 66
      " and collections of college to be used by mining school........... 90
      " appropriations for—*see* "Appropriations."
      " furnished students, accounts of, to be made to treasurer.......20, 102
      " money paid for damage to, how to be applied.................20, 103
Application to be made for power to acquire certain lands.................. 140
      " for transfer from class to class, conditions for.................. 144

Appropriations, permanent:
  for classification of Smithsonian minerals.............................. 137
  " college societies 33, 137
  " commencement, college...13, 24, 33
      "   " law school 34
  " contingencies, college...19, 33

Appropriations permanent : PAGE
    for contingencies, law school.. 34
    "   "   mining school.. 34
    " department of analytical chemistry............................12, 34
    "   "   botany...12, 33
    "   "   chemistry...............................13, 19, 21, 33
    "   "   civil engineering.. 34
    "   "   classics...12, 33
    "   "   drawing... 34
    "   "   english..12, 33
    "   "   geodesy and surveying............................ 33
    "   "   geology..12, 34
    "   "   mathematics..12, 33
    "   "   mechanics, etc..12, 33
    "   "   metallurgy..12, 34
    "   "   mineralogy...12, 34
    "   "   mining engineering................................ 34
    "   "   palæontology.. 34
    "   "   physics....................................12, 13, 33
    " endowment fund, school of mines (conditional).................... 97
    " expenses of clerk's office... 34
    "   "   real estate.. 35
    "   "   treasurer's office... 33
    " furniture of president's house... 35
    " insurance.. 33
    " interest... 35
    " library, college...13, 33
    "   "   law school...34, 68, 72
    "   "   mining school... 34
    " metallurgic laboratory... 34
    " paying water tax on president's house.............................. 166
    " printing and advertising, college.................................12, 33
    "   "   "   law school.............................34, 68
    "   "   "   mining school.....................13, 34
    " printing annual catalogue... 18
    " prizes, college..33, 57, 110, 116, 117
    "   "   law school..34, 67, 72
    "   "   mining school... 34
    "   "   university course (proposed)............................ 52
    " rent of law school building.. 34
    " repairs, college.. 33
    "   "   law school... 34
    "   "   mining school... 34
    " salaries—*see* "Appropriations for salaries."
    " scholarships and fellowships... 33
    " supplies, college...12, 33
    "   "   law school... 34
    "   "   mining school...13, 34
    " taxes.. 35

INDEX.

Appropriations for salaries and wages :   PAGE
  of adjunct professor of mathematics..................128, 129, 130, 131, 132
  " assistant in department of chemistry.......................19, 21, 22, 87
  "   "   "   analytical chemistry..............100, 106, 132
  "   "   "   geology 107, 132
  "   "   "   mineralogy........................106, 132
  "   "   "   mining engineering..............100, 106, 132
  " assistant janitor, college..128, 129
  "   "   "   school of mines................................. 131
  " chaplain...128, 129, 131, 132
  " clerk of trustees.......................................128, 129, 131, 132
  " curator of botanical collection.................................... 43
  " dean of school of mines..130, 133
  " fencing master... 89
  " instructor in elocution (proposed)................................. 27
  "   "   french (proposed)..................................... 132
  "   "   german (proposed).................................... 132
  " instructors in post-graduate course.............................60, 63
  " janitor, college...128, 129, 131, 132
  "   "   school of law.. 131
  "   "   school of mines..100, 131
  " librarian, college.......................................76, 127, 128, 129
  "   "   school of mines....................................107, 132
  " organist 128, 129, 131, 132
  " president 127, 128, 129, 130, 131, 132
  " professor of analytical chemistry........................100, 130, 132
  "   "   astronomy.. 127
  "   "   chemistry 118, 128, 129, 130, 131, 132
  "   "   constitutional history and public law.................74, 129
  "   "   elocution... 26
  "   "   evidences of christianity.........................128, 129
  " professors, "the four principal"................................. 127
  " professor of geology and palæontology............................ 132
  "   "   german 128, 129, 130, 131, 132
  "   "   greek 127, 128, 129, 130, 131, 132
  "   "   history and political economy..................118, 128, 129
  "   "   latin........................127, 128, 129, 130, 131, 132
  "   "   mathematics.. 118
  "   "   "   (higher).........................120, 128, 129
  "   "   "   (pure) 120
  "   "   mathematics and astronomy..........128, 129, 130, 131, 132
  "   "   medical jurisprudence................................. 73
  "   "   mineralogy and metallurgy.......................100, 132
  "   "   mining engineering...............................100, 132
  "   "   moral and intellectual philosophy, 118, 128, 129, 130, 131, 132
  "   "   municipal law.. 72
  "   "   physics 127, 128, 129, 130, 131, 132
  " rector of grammar school (conditional)............................ 39
  " registrar, school of mines....................................107, 132

Appropriations for salaries and wages :   PAGE
  of secretary of president.................................112, 128, 129, 131
  " servant in chemical laboratory............................19, 21, 22, 129
  " teacher in grammar school (conditional)......................... 39
  " treasurer.......................................127, 128, 129, 131, 132
  " tutors..128, 131, 132, 152

Appropriations, special :
  for accommodations of college societies............................. 137
  " apparatus, to be bought by prof. M'Culloh........................ 11
  " apparatus and books, to be bought by president................... 11
  " apparatus and chemicals, to be bought by prof. Joy................ 21
  " assistant to professor of chemistry...........................19, 21
  " astronomical observatory (asked)................................ 111
  " bats, etc., for students.. 138
  " chemical cabinet.. 19
  " contingent expenses, department of chemistry 19
  " classification of Smithsonian minerals.......................... 137
  " diagrams, etc., for university course........................... 61
  " donations to foreign schools of science.......................... 94
  " drawings, etc., to illustrate lectures on anatomy 73
  " duties and charges upon certain objects.......................... 11
  " enclosing lot in Greenwood cemetery.............................. 42
  " engraving and transferring college seal......................... 134
  " erecting building for school of mines........................... 106
  " expenses of committee of inquiry................................. 47
  " expenses of university course................................. 60, 63
  " fitting up building for school of mines.....................100, 101
  " fitting up cases for geological and mineralogical specimens....91, 101, 107
  " fitting up room for keeper of meteorological observations........ 87
  " fitting up working laboratory.................................... 46
  " furnishing fencing room....................................... 88, 89
  " furniture for president's house................................. 112
  " furniture, etc., for school of mines............................. 94
  " grammar school (provisional) 39
  " graduates to college officers................................... 129
  " instruction in elocution... 27
  " Labrador expedition.. 11
  " maps, chart, etc.. 10, 101
  " moving and arranging herbarium................................... 43
  " plans of college buildings....................................... 16
  " planting trees... 16
  " portraits of emeritus professors................................ 125
  " preserving certain grounds from washing.......................... 16
  " refunding portions of salary deducted........................... 129
  " safe and desk for the clerk..................................... 109
  " salaries of instructors in university course..................... 60
  " salary of fencing master... 89
  " small expenses, school of mines................................. 103

INDEX.

Appropriations, special :   PAGE
    for support of school of mines....................................99, 100, 101
    " surveying instruments, etc.. 11
    " temporary increase of salaries.................................131, 132
    " transcribing minutes of the trustees................................ 109
    " visiting observatories... 10
Architecture, propriety of instruction in, referred......................... 56
Arrears of assessments, standing committee to look after.................. 141
Arrears of rent, to be compounded for in certain cases..................141, 143
    " treasurer to collect.. 144
Artistic and professional schools proposed................................ 51
Arts, bachelor of, fee for degree of.. 30
    " " degree of, proposed.. 53
Arts, master of, degree of, proposed for graduate's university course........ 56
    " " fee for degree of.......................................25, 30
Assignment of subjects to the several professors........................... 119
Assistant in drawing..100, 106
    " general chemistry..19, 21, 27
    " geology.. 106
    " mineralogy.. 106
Assistants in analytical chemistry.................................100, 106, 132
    " honorary, president may appoint................................ 106
Assistant janitor, college...128, 129
    " " school of mines.. 131
Associates of the committee on school of mines......................... 95, 98
Association of the alumni, prize of...................................... 116
    " " free scholarships for 158
Astronomical observatory..111, 112
Astronomy, inquiry as to substituting tutor in mathematics for professor of.. 52
Attendance at prayers, required of the faculty............................ 14
    " " of the faculty, to be reported............................ 112
    " " required during examination 9
    " " application for excuse from, denied....................... 156
Attendance, daily, four hours of, required from certain classes...........117, 118
    " " hours of, to be distributed................................. 118
Attendance, number of hours of, for the several classes.................... 54
    " " " for professors with full salaries................ 55
Attendance on laboratory, appropriation for...........................19, 21
    " " how to be paid for..20, 21
Attendance, schemes of...............54, 55, 56, 57, 58, 61, 62, 64, 74, 110
Attorneys, treasurer authorized to employ in certain cases 145
Authority for holding meetings of trustees inquired into..............150, 151

Bachelor of arts, degree of, proposed...................................... 53
    " philosophy, degree of, proposed............................... 105
    " science, degree of, proposed.................................. 53
Badges of honorary distinctions, report on................................ 10
Bequest of Dr. William B. Moffat... 135
Bills for mining school to be paid by dean in certain cases................ 103

INDEX.

	PAGE
Bills for certain expenses to be audited by standing committee	141
Bills for ordinary supplies, standing committee to direct payment of	140
Board of the college, minutes of, not read at special meetings of trustees	149
" " tutors to have a seat at, on certain occasions	152
" " tutors to have no vote in	152

Board of trustees—*see* "Trustees."

Bonds of the college, treasurer given certain discretionary power respecting	141
Bonds, stocks, etc., treasurer to receive interest on	145
Books, donation of, from Dr. Torrey	43
Books, donations of, to be entered in a book	82
Books, library, by whom allowed to be taken	75, 78
" " number of, allowed to be taken	79
" " time allowed to be kept	79
" " professors not restricted as to number and time	79, 82
" " not to be taken without consent of librarian	80
" " of value and of reference, not to be taken	80
" " to be returned by seniors before graduation	80
" " to be returned before commencement	80
" " not to be taken out during summer vacation	81
" " professors may keep out during summer vacation	81, 82
" " catalogue of, to be kept by librarian	81
" " transfer of certain, to school of mines	95
Botanical collection of Dr. Torrey accepted	43
" " curator for, authorized	43
" " expenditures for	12, 33
Botanical garden property	14, 15, 16
" " " petition to inclose part of, as playground	138
Botany, lectures on, proposed	43
Building, extension of time for, to certain tenants	142
Building for astronomical observatory, committee on site for	111, 112
Building for law school, rent of	34, 72
Building for mining school, to be fitted up	100, 101
" " " new one to be erected	106
Building of Mr. Cooper's, offered for university course	54
Buildings, college, space for, in botanical garden property	14
" " plans of permanent	16
" " temporary to be provided	16
" " site for, to be designated in botanical garden property	17
" " site for, to be elsewhere sought	17
" " not to be used for extra academical purposes	17
" " necessity of providing new, to be kept in view	32
" " repairs of	33, 34, 126
" " to be erected with reference to enlarged course	50
" " to be erected when finances admit	50
" " part of new, for scientific purposes	51
" " part of new, to be fire-proof	51
" " scientific part of university course to be given at	60
Burial ground in Greenwood cemetery accepted	41

INDEX. 173

	PAGE
Burial ground in Greenwood cemetery, president to select	42
" " " to be fenced	42
" " " burials in	42
Business, order of, at meetings of trustees	146
Calculus, differential and integral, study of made optional	64
Cases and drawers for school of mines, appropriation for	91, 101, 107
Catalogue, annual, of the college	18
" of alumni, etc., of the college	17, 18
" of apparatus to be made	66
Chair of De Witt Clinton	156
Chaplain, salary of	128, 129, 131, 132
Chemicals, appropriations for—*see* "Appropriations."	
Chemistry, analytical, professor Joy allowed to instruct in	20, 21
" " appointment of professor recommended	90
" " chair of, established	100
" " professor of, to have charge of mining school library	95
" " salary of professor of	100, 130, 132
" " assistants in	100, 106, 132
" " professor of, to submit certain accounts to treasurer	102
" " appropriations for department of	12, 34, 101, 102
" elementary, course of, for sophomore class	118
" " professorship of, established	118
" general, appropriations for department of	13, 19, 20, 21, 22, 33, 46
" " assistant in	19, 21, 22, 87
" " instruction in, in mining school	99
Church site in botanical garden property	14, 22
Civil engineer, degree of, proposed	108
" engineering, appropriation for department of	34
" " course of, recommended	108
Class, application for transfer to higher, how to be made	144
" fee for transfer to higher	30
Classical department, appropriations for	12, 33
" " increase of time allotted to	64
" " tutor in	152
Clerk of library committee, librarian to be	76, 77
" president, salary of	112, 131, 133
" trustees, appropriation for office of	34
" " salary of	128, 129, 131, 132
" " to affix college seal—*see* "Seal."	
" " to report permanent rules, etc., of trustees	149
" " to send notice to absent trustees	145
" " to give notice of expiration of term of committee members	139
Clinton, De Witt, chair of, presented	156, 157
" Hall Association, free scholarships of, revoked	134
Collection of prayers to be prepared for college use	163
Collections, mineralogical and geological, to be rearranged	19
" " " cases for	91, 101, 107

174 INDEX.

PAGE

Collections, mineralogical and geological, donations of....................92, 93
    "   "   " possibility of acquiring certain.... 107
    "   scientific, room for, in new college buildings.................. 51
    "   " of college, to be used by mining school............... 90
College board—*see* "Board of the college."
    " bonds, treasurer given certain discretion respecting................. 141
    " buildings—*see* "Buildings, college."
    " committees on the—*see* "Committees."
    " expediency of removal of......................................48, 162
    " instruction—*see* "Instruction."
    " seal—*see* "Seal."
    " societies, appropriation for...................................33, 137
    "   " to be represented at semi-annual exhibition............... 24
    "   " to have room for their libraries......................... 138
    " of physicians and surgeons, proposal of union with................. 84
    "   "   " modification of charter necessary....... 85
    "   "   " charter of, modified................... 86
    "   "   " adopted as medical department......... 87
    "   "   " time of union with, how determined.... 86
    "   "   " union with, not to affect independence of
        college.. 86
Collegiate occupations, professors not to engage in other than...........121–123
Commencement, committee of trustees to superintend..................... 24
    " expenses of...12, 24, 33, 34
Commercial and physical geography, professorship of, proposed............ 52
Committees :
Committee on procuring site for college 17
    " on voluntary mode of instruction in chemistry.................. 19
    " on excursions of senior class, report of........................ 22
    " on commencement...23, 24
    " of visitation of the college........................ ....28, 29, 151
    " on expediency of abolishing intermediate examination.........., 29
    " on a financial policy.......... ....31, 161
    " on grammar school...39–41
    " of honors, established.. 44
    "   " to report upon candidates for honorary degrees........ 44
    "   " report of, on badges of distinction.................... 10
    " of inquiry into state of the college—*see* "Inquiry," etc.
    " on course of instruction—*see* "Instruction," etc.
    " on procuring accommodations for the college.................. 48
    " of conference respecting use of Cooper institute................ 54
    " on scheme of study for senior year 56
    " on propriety of instruction in architecture............. 56
    "   "   " design and drawing............... 56
    " on university course of instruction—*see* "Instruction," etc.
    " on a scheme of instruction reported by faculty............. 62
    " on a plan for instruction in astronomy............... 62
    " to prepare a scheme of study................................. 65

INDEX. 175

Committees :	PAGE
Committee on reports of professors respecting movable property	66
" on law school—*see* "Law, school of," etc.	
" on law library	67
" on prizes in the law school	70
" on library—*see* "Library," etc.	
" on library regulations	82
" of conference respecting school of medicine	84, 86
" on establishing a gymnasium	88
" on school of mines—*see* "Mines," etc.	
" on obtaining certain scientific collections	107
" on demand of regents of university for trustees' minutes	109
" on astronomical observatory	111, 112
" of conference on alumni prize	116
" on death of Dr. King and prof. Anthon	116, 117
" on expediency of abolishing certain professorships	121
" on extra collegiate occupations of professors	122
" on emeritus professors	124, 125
" on repairs	126
" on salaries	130
" on practice of holding special and stated meetings	150
" on expediency of appointing tutors	151
" on memorial to congress respecting weights, measures, and coins	154
" on expediency of removal of the college	162
" to make collection of prayers, etc	163
" on device for college seal	163, 164, 165
" standing—*see* "Standing committee."	
Committees, reports of, to be in writing	149
" special, to be appointed by the chair	149
Competitors for prizes, regulations respecting	69–71, 113–117
" for scholarships and fellowships, regulations respecting	158–161
Constitutional history and public law, chair of, established	74
" " " duties of professor of	74
" " " salary of professor of	74
Contingencies, appropriations for	19, 33, 34, 101
Contributions, amount of, to school of mines	98
" time for receiving extended	98
Convocation, university, faculty authorized to send delegates	153
Cooper union building offered for use of university course	54
Copy of trustees' minutes to be made for regents	109
Corporation, new, proposed for school of mines	96
Correspondence with foreign scientific schools authorized	94
Course of instruction—*see* "Instruction."	
" study, statute on, adopted	55
" " in school of mines, modified	108
Damage to apparatus, etc., to be paid for	20, 103
" " money received for, how to be applied	20, 103
Davies, Charles, made emeritus professor	124

INDEX.

	PAGE
Dean of school of mines, authorized	102
" " duties of	102
" " to submit certain accounts to treasurer	102
" " to be relieved of certain expenses	102
" " to pay certain bills	103
" " salary of	131, 133
Declamation, prizes for, abolished	31, 116
Degrees, honorary, expenses of, to be defrayed by the trustees	25
" " diplomas for, to be issued	25
" " committee on	44
" " how conferred	44
" " standing committee to report candidates for	139
Degree of bachelor of arts, fee for diploma	25, 30
" " proposal to bestow	53
" " candidates for, to comply with certain conditions	80
" " laws, upon whom to be conferred	68, 71, 74
" " diploma to be issued for	71
" " diploma, how signed	71
" " philosophy, proposed	105
" " science, proposed	53
" doctor of medicine, upon whom to be conferred	85
" " how conferred	86
" " diplomas for, how signed	86
" doctor of philosophy, proposed	105
" of engineer of mines, fee for	26
" master of arts, fee required for	25, 26, 30
" " for graduates of university course	56
" master of laws, on whom conferred	74
Degrees in the school of mines	104, 105, 108, 109
" proposed at end of supplemental course	51
Delinquents in paying tuition fees, to be reported	29, 112
Departments of instruction, bills for, to be audited before paid	141
" " appropriations for—*see* "Appropriations."	
" " balance of appropriations for, how disposed of.	12, 13, 33, 34
" " professors in, to control appropriations for.	10, 11, 12, 19, 101
" " seniors, given choice of three	55
" " option of three for seniors, abolished	63
Deposit required from students using collections	20, 103
" " " " how disposed of	21, 103
Design and drawing, propriety of establishing chair of	56
Desk for filing papers for clerk of trustees	109
Device for college seal	133, 163, 164, 165
Diagrams for certain departments	73, 101
Diplomas—*see* "Degrees."	
Discipline, defective, cause to be inquired into	47
Doctor of philosophy, degree of, proposed	105

INDEX.

	PAGE
Donations of minerals to school of mines	92, 93
" money " " amount of	98
" to be made to foreign schools of science	94
" to library, list of, to be kept	82
Drawers and cases for mining school, appropriations for	101
Drawing, assistant in	100, 106, 132
" appropriation for department of	34, 101
" instruction in, to be given by adjunct prof. of mathematics	57, 120
" free hand, in university course	57
" and design, propriety of establishing chair of	56
Duties of certain professors	118
Dwelling house for Dr. Torrey to be put in order	43
" " " allowed longer use of	43
Education, professors to suggest improvements on college plan of	49
" science and art of, to be taught	59
" for other particulars concerning—*see* "Instruction."	
Egleston, professor, communication from, referred	89
" " authorized to visit Washington	136
Elective study, three courses of, for senior class	55, 63
Elocution, instruction in	26, 27, 28, 153
" professor of	26, 27
Emeritus professors	123, 124, 125
Endowment fund, proposed for school of mines	97
Engineering, civil, appropriation for department of	34
" mining, " "	34, 101
" " professor of, to be nominated	92
" " " salary of	100, 132
" " assistant in	100, 106, 132
" railway, to be taught	99
Engineer of mines, degree of	105, 108
" " " fee for	26
English department, appropriation for	12, 33
" literature, tutor in, appointed	152
" seminary prize	115
Equipments, etc., for mining school, appropriation for	94
Ethics, propriety of division of department into three	53
Evidences of religion, by whom to be taught	113, 118, 119
Examinations, daily prayers to be continued during	9
" professors to attend all	9
" gowns to be worn at	9
" committee of trustees to attend	28, 29
" intermediate, proposal to abolish	29, 157
" in university course	60
" for degrees in law school	68, 71, 74
" for prizes in law school	69–71
" for degrees in mining school	105
" for seminary prizes	114, 115

178   INDEX.

	PAGE
Examinations for prizes in german	116
" for prizes in greek	117
" for honors proposed	157
" for fellowships and scholarships, proposed	159, 161
Excursions of senior class, allowed for certain purposes	22
Exercises in open air for students, appropriation for	138
Exhibition, semi-annual, college societies to be represented in	24
" " abolished	24, 31, 116
Exhibitions for public declamation	24, 26
" " " faculty and trustees to attend	24, 26
" appropriations for	33
Expenditures for departments, professors to control	10, 11, 12, 19, 101
" " must be approved by president	12
" for library, to be directed by library committee	13, 77
" " must be approved by the president	83
" " limited	127
" for botanical garden property, to be reported	14
" for working laboratory, how to be met	20
" on account of damage to apparatus, etc., how met	20, 103
" for honorary degrees, defrayed by the trustees	25
" necessary to obtain degree of master of arts	25, 26, 30
" for instruction in elocution, how met	26, 28
" attending transfer to a higher class	30
" for grammar school, how to be met	38, 40
" of the committee of inquiry, to be paid by the trustees	47
" for advertising university course, how met in certain cases	63
" on account of law library, control of	67
" for publishing names of prize men	71
" for law school, expediency of, how decided	73
" on account of the general library, control of	83
" for gymnastic exercises, inquiry respecting	89
" on account of school of mines, control of	101
" for expenses and other charges, school of mines	103
" for portraits of emeritus professors, to be met by the college	123
" for repairing professors' houses, how paid	126
" on account of prof. Egleston's visit to Washington, how paid	137
" for agent of upper estates, how directed	142
" on account of diplomas and tuition—*see* "Fees."	
" for other expenditures and expenses—*see* "Appropriations."	
Expulsion of professor M'Culloh	120
Faculty, college, empowered to require students to wear gowns	9
" " to attend examinations in gowns	9
" " to attend daily prayers	14
" " attendance of, at daily prayers, to be reported	112
" " to attend public exhibitions	24, 26
" " authorized to open a grammar school	38
" " opinions of, respecting university education, to be taken	46
" " members of, to suggest improvements in plan of education	49

	PAGE
Faculty, college, members of, exempt from certain library regulations..	79, 81, 82
" " certain members of, to have seats in faculty of mines.......	100
" " to report on expediency of a military department..........	88
" " suggest erection of a gymnasium	88
" " authorized to send delegates to university convocation	153
" " to prepare memorial on uniform system of weights, etc.....	154
" " sons of members of, exempt from payment of tuition money.	158
" of law to be established	72
" " to be named in annual catalogue	18
" of medicine, to be named in annual catalogue	18
" of mines, certain college professors to have seats in	100
" " dean of—*see* "Dean."	
" " recommend certain degrees........................	104, 105
" " recommend new plan of instruction.....................	108
Fees for diplomas	25, 26, 30, 31, 128
" for matriculation	30
" of student transferred to a higher class	30
" for tuition, when due..	29
" " delinquents in paying, to be reported...................	29, 112
" " of students admitted after opening.......................	30
" " to be remitted in certain cases	30, 36
" " salaries of professors partially dependent on...............	127
" " no part of, to be received by president or professors.... ...	128
" " to be paid treasurer...................................	144
" " in law school...	72
" " " to be remitted in certain cases..............	36, 72
" " " how collected............................	72
" " " how to be applied.......................	72
" " in mining school	31
" " " " to be received by professors..............	91, 92
" " " " to be paid treasurer.....................	102
" " " " to be remitted in certain cases	31, 36, 107
" " in university course	59, 61
" " to be paid professors in certain cases.....................	63
" " in grammar school.....................................	38
" " " " how appropriated....................	38, 39
Fellowships and scholarships, appropriation for (provisional)	33
" " proposal to establish....................	158—161
" in university course provided for...........................	56
Fencing room to be fitted up..	89
" master to be engaged...	89
" certain lots, expediency of petitioning for.......................	140
Financial policy, permanent, ordinance establishing	32
" " not to prejudice law school.................	35
" " when to take effect	36
Fine for not wearing academical dress	155
Fiscal year, when to terminate	144
Fixtures for school of mines, appropriation for..........................	101

INDEX.

	PAGE
Forfeiture of leases waived in certain cases	143
Free academy to have four free scholarships	135
Free scholarships in mining school, on certain conditions	99
" " in theological seminary	114, 115
" " emeritus professor entitled to one	123
" " granted to certain schools	134
" " of Clinton hall association revoked	134
" " of New York high school, lapse of	134
" " granted to Free academy	135
" " granted the state, on conditions	135
" " founded by Dr. W. B. Moffat	135
" " granted various bodies	158
" tuition	30, 31, 36, 38, 72, 107, 158
French, professorship of, proposed	53
" classes in, to be formed when expedient	57
" professorship of, abolished	121
" and german, instructors in, for school of mines	90, 92
" " salary of instructors in, when appointed	132
" and spanish, classes, when organized, to attend two hours a week	110
Freshman class, certain members of, to have use of college library	75
Fuel and light for mining school to be furnished by the college	94
Fund, accumulating	33, 35
" endowment, for school of mines proposed	97
" Gebhard	36, 37
Furniture for president's house, appropriation for	35, 112
" etc., for mining school, appropriation for	94
Gebhard fund	36, 37
Geodesy and surveying, appropriation for department of	33
Geography, ancient, required for admission	65
" " text-book in, president to report	65
" physical and commercial, chair of, proposed	52
" " lecturer on, for university course	60
Geological collection, appropriations for cases for	91, 101, 107
" " of Dr. Newberry, possibility of acquiring	107
" surveys, certain reports of, for presentation	94
Geology, appropriations for department of	12, 34, 101
" professorship of, proposed	52
" lecturer in, for university course	60
" salary of professor of	132
" assistant in	107, 132
Geometry, analytical, made an optional study	64
German, professorship of, established	37
" scheme of voluntary attendance referred	56
" prizes in, established	57, 110, 116
" instruction in, to form part of sub-graduate course	110
" seniors and juniors allowed to have instruction in	110
" sophomores not required to attend	110

INDEX.

	PAGE
German and french, instructors in, for school of mines	90, 92
Gowns, wearing of, authorized	9
" " required	9
" professors to wear	9
" and caps, regulations respecting, adopted by students	9
" president and professors recommended to wear	155
Graduates of university course, degree for	56
" of the college, who enter university course, fees of	61
Graduation in school of mines, when to take place	108
Grammar school, established	37
" " rules for organization and government of	38
" " trustees to superintend	38
" " branches to be taught in	38
" " expenses of, how defrayed	38
" " trustees may discontinue	38
" " rate of tuition in	38
" " college board authorized to open	38
" " committee of trustees to superintend	39
" " professor Anthon made rector of	39
" " agreement with professor Anthon respecting	40
" " common school teachers to be taught in	41
" " course of instruction in, referred to committee	52
" " allowed four free scholarships	134
" " discontinued	41
Grants of land by Congress, inquiry respecting	93
Gratuitous instruction	30, 31, 36, 38, 72, 107, 158
Gratuity to certain college officers	129
Greek, department of, assigned to professor Anthon	119
" " appropriations for	12, 33
" salary of professor of—*see* "Appropriations."	
" increase of time allotted to	64
" seminary prize in, founded	114, 115
" prizes in, established	117
" tutor in	152
Greenwood cemetery, burial lot in, accepted	41
" " president to select lot in	42
" " lot in, to be enclosed	42
" " burials in	42
Gymnastic exercises, expediency of introducing	88, 89
Herbarium	42, 43
History, American, professorship of, proposed	52
" natural, " "	52
" " lyceum of, granted rooms in college	111
" and political economy assigned to professor of philosophy	65
" " " name of chair changed	74, 119
" " " expediency of abolishing chair of	121
" " " professor of, salary—*see* "Appropriations."	
" " " " transferred	73

INDEX.

	PAGE
History of mathematics to be taught	121
" of moral and intellectual philosophy to be taught	64
Honorary assistants, president may appoint	106
" degrees—*see* "Degrees."	
Honors, committee of	44
" special examination for, proposed	157
House-rent allowed professors	118, 128, 129, 130
Industrial drawing assigned to adjunct professor of mathematics	57
Inquiry into system of volunteering in chemistry	19
" into extra collegiate occupations of professors	122
" as to expediency of appointing tutors	151

Inquiry into the state of the college, committee of:

" appointment of	44
" to consider the granting of intermissions by the president	44
" to take statements of faculty and librarian on the subject	45
" to inquire into administration of college and grammar school	45
" to recommend measures for correction of defects	45
" to obtain statements and opinions respecting plan of university education	46
" recommend working laboratory for professor M'Culloh	46
" authorized to incur expenses	47
" to inquire into system of volunteering in mathematics	47
" to inquire into causes of defective discipline	47
" report of, to be printed and bound	47
" to consider the appointment of tutors	152

Instruction, course of, committee on:

" appointment of	48
" to inquire into expediency of removal of the college	48
" to inquire into necessity of changes and additions to course	48
" to inquire into expediency of furnishing rooms, etc., to students	48
" recommend removal of the college	48
" recommend that professors hold titles, etc., *ad interim*	49
" invite professors to suggest improvements on college course	49
" suggest a statute on course of instruction	49
" authorized to prepare a statute on the course	49
" recommend present course to be continued for a time	50
" recommend erection of new college buildings	50
" recommend additional professorships	50
" to consider subject of professional and scientific instruction	50, 51
" to consider subject of grammar school instruction	52
" to consider the creation of certain additional professorships	52
" to consider the awarding of prizes in university course	52
" present a statute on course of instruction	53
" report a scheme of attendance	56
" report on instruction in drawing and modern languages	57
" to consider entire subject of college instruction	64
" recommend certain branches of mathematics be made optional	64
" recommend reduction of time allotted to mathematics	64

Instruction, course of, committee on :	PAGE
" recommend increase of time allotted to classics	64
" recommend continuance of chair of physics	64
" recommend certain method of instruction in physics	64
" recommend certain method of instruction in literature and philosophy	64
Instruction, course of university, committee on :	
" appointment of	58
" report in favor of opening the several schools	58
" recommend the subjects to be taught in the schools	58
" recommend the place for giving instruction	59, 60
" recommend the amount and the disposal of fees	59, 61
" recommend the terms of instruction	59
" advise concerning the tenure of office of instructors	59
" to provide accommodations for instruction	59
" recommend the time to begin the university year	60
" to engage instructors	60
" to arrange details with professors	60
" recommend examinations in the course	60
" to procure diagrams, drawings, etc	61
" to consider expediency of a practical school of science	63
" recommend organization of a law school	66
" recommend certain subjects for instruction in law school	66, 67
" discharged	63
Instruction, course of, to be defined	49
" " present, to be continued	49
" " co-ordinate, recommended	50
" " co-ordinate, when to commence	50
" " supplemental, proposed	50
" " university, proposed	50
" " statute on university	54, 55
" " university, to whom open	56
" " scheme for university, referred to faculty	61
" " university, president to give notice of	61
" " " " to report results of	63
" " " treasurer to report expenses of	63
" " in college, referred to committee	64
" departments of, appropriations for—see "Appropriations."	
" " bills for, to be audited before paid	141
" gratuitous	33, 31, 36, 38, 72, 107
" in architecture, propriety of	55
" in botany	42
" in design and drawing, propriety of	56
" in elocution	26, 27, 28, 153
" in evidences of religion assigned to prof. moral philosophy	118
" " " " to president	113
" in grammar school	38, 52
" in history, etc., assigned to professor of philosophy	65
" in industrial drawing	57

	PAGE
Instruction in mathematics, etc., school of mines, provided for	99, 100
" in modern languages	57, 110, 132
" in railway engineering	99
" in other subjects—*see* the various departments.	
" military, department of, disapproved	88
" new plan of, for school of mines, approved	108
" terms of, in school of mines	103
" terms of, in university course	60
Instructors, additional, in law school, to be engaged only on conditions	73
" for university course	60
" in modern languages	132
Insurance, appropriation for	33
Intellectual and moral philosophy, history of, to be taught	64
" " chair of—*see* "Philosophy."	
Interest, appropriation for	35
Interest on U. S. bonds, etc., to be received by treasurer	145
Inventory of movable property to be made	66
Investment of accumulating fund	35
" of Gebhard fund	37
" of certain moneys authorized	142
Investments, certain, allowed to be converted	142
Italian, professorship in, proposed	53
Janitor and his assistant, college, salaries of	128, 129
" " school of mines, salaries of	100, 131
" school of law, salary of	131
Jay professorship of greek and latin established	117
Junior class allowed to attend instruction in german	110
Jurisprudence, elective course for seniors adopted	55
" " " abolished	63
" school for university course adopted	55
" " to whom open	56
" " subjects to be taught in	58
Kemble, Gouverneur, donation of, to school of mines	93
" " thanks to	93
" " name to be placed on each specimen presented	93, 94
Laboratory, chemical, servant in	19
" " regulations concerning	20
" metallurgic, appropriation for	34
" working, to be fitted up	46
Labrador expedition, appropriation for	11
Land grants by congress, inquiry respecting	93
Lands, application to be made for power to acquire certain	140
Language, german—*see* "German."	
Languages, ancient, title of adjunct professor of, changed	117
" " increase of time allotted to	64
" " tutors in	152
" modern, professorships of, proposed	53

INDEX.

	PAGE
Languages. modern, attendance of classes in	57, 110
Latin, department of, assigned to professor Drisler	119
Latin, department of, increase of time allotted to	64
" tutor in	152
Law, constitutional, president to teach	118
Law faculty, propriety of establishing	72
Law, professorship of, established	117
" " trustees to make regulations concerning	117
" professor of, not to attend faculty meetings	117
" municipal, professor of, secretary of law library committee	67
" " " to examine candidates for degree of LL.B.	68, 71
" " " to conduct examinations for prizes	70
" " " to collect tuition fees	72
" " " salary of	72, 73
" " " a member of the law committee	73
" " " consent necessary to employment of additional instructors	73
" " " to prevent disturbance of trustees' meetings	120
Law, school of :	
" establishment of	66
" appropriations for	34
" gratuitous lecturers in, to be secured	67
" professors of college to lecture in	67
" prizes established in	67
" committee on library of	67
" appropriations for library of	68
" regulations concerning examinations and prizes in	68—71
" graduates of, to have degree of bachelor of laws	68, 71, 74
" seal of college to be affixed to certificates and diplomas	71
" system of prizes in, modified	72
" faculty to be established	72
" regulations for the support of	72, 73
" fees for tuition in	72
" " by whom collected	72
" " to be paid into treasury	72
" " to be remitted in certain cases	72
" " how to be applied	72
" rent and repairs to be paid out of the general fund	72
" expediency of expenditures for, to be decided by trustees	73
" additional instructors in, to be employed only on conditions	73
" elementary anatomy and physiology to be taught in	73
" salary of professor of medical jurisprudence in	73
" professor Lieber transferred to faculty of	73
" title of professor Lieber's chair in	74
" duties of professor Lieber in	74
" salary of professor Lieber in	74
" examination in, for degree of master of laws	74
" meetings of trustees held at	146
" warden of, to have trustees' table cleared of books, etc.	166

	PAGE
Law, school of, committee on :	
" appointment of...	67
" to determine details of prizes..	67
" report regulations for examinations and prizes......................	68
" to select a committee on prizes	70
" to attend concluding examination of the senior class.................	71
" to consider the establishment of a law faculty	72
" professor of municipal law a member of.............................	73
" to recommend expenditures...	73
" authorized to allow lectures on anatomy, etc........................	73
" to determine title and duties of professor Lieber's chair..............	73, 74
" to prescribe requisites for degrees of LL.B. and LL.M................	73, 74
" to prevent interruption of trustees' meetings.......................	166
" to provide closets for books, etc., of law students...................	166
Laws, degree of bachelor of, on whom conferred	68, 71, 74
" degree of master of, on whom conferred...........................	74
" body of, for the college to be prepared	163
Leases to be made of lots in botanical garden property.	14, 15, 16
" transfer of, standing committee authorized to consent to.........	139, 141
" surrender of, authorized in certain cases........................	141, 143
" modification of, allowed in certain cases.........................	142
" forfeiture of, waived in certain cases..............................	143
" of lots in upper estate, left to standing committee..................	143
Lecturers in university course...	55, 60
" gratuitous, in law school...	66, 67
Lectures on anatomy, etc., offer of a course in college declined...	65
" " " to be given in law school......................	73
Legislature to be applied to, for power to acquire certain lands	140
Letters, elective course of, for seniors, adopted...........................	55
" " " " abolished	63
" school of, for university course, adopted.........................	55
" " subjects to be taught in.............................	58, 59
" " lectures in, where given......	59, 60
Librarian of the college, to be secretary of library committee	76, 77
" " " salary of......................................	76
" " " annual report of..................	77, 78, 81, 83
" " " to observe and enforce the rules of library.........	78
" " " to collect fines for detention of books.............	79
" " " to keep account of books delivered and received....	79
" " " to observe condition of books returned	80
" " " to have every library book in its place before commencement....	81
" " " to see to the care of the library room..............	81
" " " to prevent loud conversation in library............	81
" " " to arrange the books upon the shelves.............	81
" " " to keep a correct and complete catalogue..........	81
" " " to keep a list of donations of books...............	82
Librarian of the school of mines to be appointed..........................	107

	PAGE

Libraries of the college societies to have room in college................... 138
Library, college, committee on :
"   appointment of... 75
"   duties of..75, 77
"   authorized to make regulations..............................75, 76, 77
"   authorized to dispose of duplicates of works.................75, 76, 77
"   reconstruction of.. 76
"   times of meeting of...76, 77
"   quorum of... 76
"   librarian to be secretary of......................................76, 77
"   consent necessary to all debts for library.......................76, 78
"   to be elected by ballot... 76
"   members of, to serve three years.................................. 77
"   vacancies in, how filled.. 77
"   regulations established by.. 78
"   report against modification of rules in favor of professors.......... 83
"   president to be a permanent member of............................ 83
Library, college, appropriations for.......................................13, 33
"   "   to be used by whom... 75
"   "   no debts to be contracted for, without consent............76, 78
"   "   purchase of books for, by whom directed.................. 77
"   "   control of expenditures for..............................77, 83
"   "   condition of, to be annually reported...................... 77
"   "   regulations for..78—83
"   "   catalogue of books in, to be kept......................... 81
"   "   list of donations to, to be kept........................... 82
"   "   state of, to be inquired into.............................. 82
"   "   certain books of, transferred to mining school library...... 95
Library, law school, appropriations for..................................34, 68
"   "   committee on.. 67
Library, mining school, appropriation for................................... 34
"   "   "   certain books transferred to........................ 95
"   "   "   professor of chemistry to have charge of............ 95
"   "   "   "   "   to be responsible for......... 95
"   "   "   by whom to be used............................... 95
"   "   "   accommodations for, to be provided................ 96
"   "   "   librarian for, to be appointed..................... 107
Lieber, professor, subjects assigned to..................................... 119
"   "   transferred to faculty of law............................ 73
"   "   subjects assigned to, in law school...................... 74
"   "   salary of, in law school............................74, 129
"   "   salary of, to be paid out of general fund................ 130
Light to be furnished school of mines by the college....................... 94
Literary societies, appropriations for..................................33, 137
"   "   to have representatives at exhibitions.................... 24
"   "   to have room in college for libraries.................... 138
Literature, ancient and modern, chair of, united with another.............. 119
"   english, tutor in... 152

	PAGE
Literature, modern, history of, to be taught.	64
Loan authorized to regulate botanical garden property	14, 15
Logic to be taught by professor of moral philosophy.	118
Losses of books, garments, etc., college not to be responsible.	23
Lots, expediency of petitioning for fencing certain.	140
" leases of—*see* "Leases."	
Lyceum of natural history allowed rooms in college	111
McCulloh, professor, authorized to purchase apparatus.	11
" " " fit up a working laboratory	46
" " expelled	120
McVickar, professor, prizes founded by	114
Maps of botanical garden property to be made	14, 15
" charts, etc., appropriation for	10
" and diagrams for school of mines, appropriation for	101
Mathematics, appropriations for department of	12, 33
" system of volunteering in, to be inquired into	47
" expediency of tutor in, instead of a professor of astronomy	52
" certain branches of, made optional	64
" hours allotted to, in junior year, reduced	64
" adjunct professor of, to teach drawing	57, 120
" adjunct professor of, made professor of pure	120
" professor of, made professor of higher	120
" emeritus professor of	123
" tutor in	152
" salaries of professors—*see* "Appropriations."	
" higher, professor of, to lecture on history of mathematics	121
" " expediency of abolishing chair of	121
" pure, in mining school, by whom taught	100
" and astronomy, professor of, to teach mechanics	65, 100
" " " emeritus professor of	123
Master of laws, degree of	74
Mechanics and astronomy, appropriation for department of	12, 33
" assigned to professor of mathematics and astronomy	65
" in school of mines, by whom taught	100
Medals, system of awarding abolished	127
Medical jurisprudence, professor of, salary	72
" " " to lecture on anatomy, etc	73
" " appropriation for department of	73
Medicine, school of,	84, 85, 86
" degree of doctor of, upon whom conferred	85
" " " how conferred	86
Meetings of trustees, absence from five successive, forfeits seat.	145
" " time of	145, 146, 150
" " place of	145, 146, 150
" " rules of order at	146
" " practice of holding, referred to committee.	150
" " not to be interrupted	120, 166

INDEX.

	PAGE
Memorial in favor of uniform system of weights, etc.	154
Merit rolls	18, 87
Metallurgic laboratory, appropriations for	34
Metallurgy, appropriation for department of	34, 101
Metaphysics, pure, study of, to be reduced	64
Meteorological observations to be kept	87
Microscope, instruction in use of, proposed	43
Military education, department of, disapproved	88
Mineralogical collection of prof. Egleston, possibility of acquiring	107
" specimens, cases for, to be provided	91, 101
Mineralogy and geology, professorship of, recommended	91
" and metallurgy, professor of, to be nominated	92
" " salary of professor of	100, 132
" " assistant in	106
" appropriation for department of	34, 101
Minerals, donations of, to school of mines	92, 93
" appropriation for	101
" agreement with Smithsonian institute respecting	136
" appropriation for classification of Smithsonian	137

Mines, school of, committee on:
- " appointment of 90
- " recommend rooms to be set apart for school 90, 91
- " recommend appointment of professors without salary 90, 91
- " recommend the use of college collections by the school 90
- " recommend appointment of a professor of mineralogy and geology.... 91
- " to prepare rules and regulations 91
- " to nominate instructors 92
- " to advertise opening of the school 92
- " to make inquiry respecting land grants by congress 93
- " to procure furniture and equipments for the school 94
- " to have associates 95, 98
- " to consider expediency of a new corporation 96
- " report against a new corporation 96
- " recommend appropriation to support the school 96
- " propose to raise endowment fund 97
- " quorum of 98
- " manner of voting in 98
- " report amount of contributions to the school 98
- " to contract for erection of a building 106
- " to consider new plan of instruction 108
- " report in favor of new plan of instruction 108

Mines, school of:
- " expediency of establishing, referred 89
- " establishment of 91
- " professor of mineralogy and geology to be appointed 91
- " appropriation for cases in 91, 107
- " certain professors to be appointed 92
- " donations of minerals to 92, 93

INDEX.

	PAGE
Mines, opening to be advertised	92
" appropriations for	34, 91, 94, 96, 97, 100, 101, 106, 107

Mines, school of :
- " foreign correspondence on account of, authorized 94
- " donations by, to be made to foreign schools 94
- " certain books to be transferred to library of 95
- " library of, to be under charge of professor of chemistry 95
- " library of, by whom to be used 95
- " proposed new corporation for 96
- " entitled to support 97
- " endowment fund proposed 97
- " amount of contributions received for 98
- " time for receiving contributions for, extended 98
- " instruction in railway engineering to be given 99
- " free scholarships in, on certain conditions 99
- " instruction in physics, etc., by whom given 99, 100
- " title of chair of chemistry in, changed 100
- " certain college professors to have seats in faculty of 100
- " building to be fitted up for 100
- " control of expenditures for 101, 102
- " accounts for breakage and supplies to be made to treasurer ... 102
- " money received for breakage, how to be applied 102, 103
- " dean of—*see* " Dean."
- " deposit required from students using collections 103
- " terms of instruction in 103
- " vacations in 103
- " degrees in 104, 105, 108, 109
- " fee for degree in 26
- " building to be erected for 106
- " assistants in 100, 106, 107, 132
- " honorary assistants in, president may appoint 106
- " registrar and librarian, to be appointed 107
- " possibility of acquiring certain collections for 107
- " gratuitous instruction in, to certain students 107
- " new plan of instruction for, adopted 108
- " salaries of instructors in—*see* "Appropriations."

Mining and metallurgy, professorship of, recommended 90
- " engineering, appropriation for department of 34, 101
- " " professor of, to be nominated 92
- " " salary of professor of 100, 132
- " " assistant in 100, 106, 132

Minutes of the college board, to be read at stated meetings of trustees 146
- " " not to be read at special meetings of trustees .. 149
- " " to be inspected by committee of visitation 154
- " of standing committee, to be read at stated meetings of trustees 139
- " " " not to be read at special meeting of trustees. 149
- " of board of trustees, demanded by regents of university 109
- " " " demand for, not complied with 109

INDEX. 191

	PAGE
Minutes of board of trustees, copy from 1784 to 1787 for regents	109
" " " to be transcribed	109
" " " report to regents not to be entered on	151
Models for astronomical department, appropriation for	10
" for school of mines, appropriation for	101
Modern languages, professorships in, proposed	53
" " attendance of classes in	57, 110
" " instructors in, for school of mines	90, 92
" literature, history of, to be taught	64
Modification of certain leases to be allowed	141
Moffat scholarships	135
Moral and intellectual philosophy, history of, to be taught	64
" " " prof. of, to teach hist. and polit. econ.	66
" " " " " evidences, and logic	118
" " " subjects to be taught in department of	119
" " " salary of prof. of—*see* "Appropriations."	
Movable property, inventory of, to be made	66
Municipal law, professor of—*see* "Law."	
Natural history, lyceum of, to have rooms in the college	111
" " professorship of, proposed	52
New corporation of school of mines proposed	96
Observatories, appropriation for visiting	10
Observatory, astronomical	111, 112
Occupations, professors not to engage in other than collegiate	121, 123
Office, tenure of, for instructors in university course	59, 60
Order, rules of, for meetings of trustees	146—149
Order of business at meetings of trustees	146
Ordinances, observance of, to be reported upon by standing committee	139
Organist, salary of	128, 129, 131, 132
Palæontology, appropriation for department of	34
Papers of board of trustees to be marked and indexed	109
Parents failing to pay tuition fees of sons, to be reported	112
Party walls, agreement for erection of, to be made with tenants	142
Penalty for not wearing academic dress	155
Permanent financial policy	32
Philosophy, degree of bachelor of	105, 108
" " doctor of, proposed	105
" moral and intellectual, history of, to be taught	64
" " " subjects assigned to department of	119
" " " professor of, to teach evidences of Christianity and logic	118
" " " chair of, united with another	119
" natural, and chemistry, professor of, to keep meteorological observations	87
Physical apparatus, appropriation for purchase of	11
Physical and commercial geography, professorship of, proposed	52

INDEX.

	PAGE
Physical and natural science, annual advancement proposed to be reported..	52
Physics, department of, appropriation for............................12, 13, 33	
" " expediency of abolishing referred..................	64
" " to be continued	64
" " subjects assigned to	119
" " subjects in, to be taught without use of calculus.....	64
" " text-books to be used in..........................	64
Physics, in school of mines, by whom to be taught	99
Physiology and anatomy, proposed course of, in college, declined..........	65
" " elementary, to be taught in law school............	73
Physiology and natural history, professorship of, proposed..................	52
Place of meeting of trustees...145, 150	
Plan of instruction for the mining school adopted........................	108
Political economy assigned to professor of philosophy and literature	65
Portraits of emeritus professors to be painted............................	123
" " " to be formally introduced into the college ...	125
Post graduate course—*see* "Instruction."	
Practical chemistry, department of, discontinued	19
Prayers, collection of, committee to make................................	163
" daily, to be said during examinations............................	9
" faculty to attend..	14
" attendance of faculty at, to be reported	112
" application for excuse from, denied.............................	156
Preparatory year in school of mines established............................	108
President authorized to purchase apparatus and books....................	11
" " to prepare general catalogue of the college...........17, 18	
" to see that conveniences for cloaks, etc., are furnished............	23
" with committee of trustees to make arrangements for commencement.	24
" to receive fees for diplomas	25
" to make arrangements for instruction in elocution 27, 153	
" to report names of delinquents in paying tuition fees 29, 112	
" with treasurer allowed to remit tuition fees......................	30
" to make publication concerning free tuition	36
" to select lot in Greenwood cemetery and enclose it	42
" to give permits for burial in college lot..........................	42
" discretionary power of, concerning intermissions, inquiry about....	44
" to report resolutions concerning working laboratory to faculty.....	46
" to report schemes of attendance—*see* "Attendance."	
" to give notice of university course of instruction..................	61
" to report results of university course	63
" to report text-book in ancient geography	65
" to obtain catalogue of apparatus belonging to college	66
" a member of law library committee.............................	67
" to allow use of library to certain members of freshman class.......	75
" a member of committee on college library.................. ....76, 83	
" to control expenditures for college library.......................	83
" to assist in conferring degrees in medical department............85, 86	
" to sign diplomas for degree of doctor of medicine...............85, 86	

INDEX.

	PAGE
President to transmit merit rolls to parents	87
" report of, on military education	88
" authorized to employ a fencing master	89
" authorized to purchase copies of reports for presentation	94
" report of, on providing for instruction in mining school	99
" to control general expenditures for mining school	101
" report of, on degrees in school of mines	104
" authorized to permit certain mining students to attend without charge	107
" to report attendance of faculty at prayers	112
" appropriation to furnish house of	35, 112
" authorized to employ a secretary	112
" to instruct in the evidences of religion	113
" to have direction of tutor in rhetoric and belles-lettres	118
" to report on extra collegiate occupations of professors	121, 122
" not to receive any portion of tuition fees	128
" with treasurer, to have college seal engraved and transferred	134
" to provide accommodations for college societies	137
" to report on expediency of suppressing secret societies	138
" to report on applications for transfer from class to class	144
" not to be a member of committee of visitation	154
" report of, concerning the intermediate examination	157
" reports resolutions on prize fellowships and scholarships	158
" annual water-tax on house of, to be paid by treasurer	166
" salary of—see "Appropriations for salaries."	
Printing, appropriations for	12, 33, 34, 68, 101
Prizes, college, appropriation for	33
" in declamation, discontinued	24, 31, 116
" in german established	57, 110, 116
" in greek established	117
" seminary, founded by Dr. McVickar	114
" " regulations concerning	114, 115
" " privileges of successful candidates for	115
" " payment of, by whom made	115
" " amount of, if not bestowed, specially appropriated	116
" of the alumni association	116
" law school, appropriation for	34, 67
" " regulations concerning	68—72
" " to consist of what	71
" " committee on, of whom composed	70
" " system of, modified	72
" mining school, appropriation for	34
Prize fellowships, proposal to establish	158
" " to be open to whom	158
" " examinations for	159
" scholarship in theological seminary granted the college	113
" scholarships in university course, appropriation for, proposed	52
" " " " provided for	56

INDEX.

	PAGE
Prize scholarships and prizes	113
" " proposal to establish three	160
" " to be open to whom	160, 161
" " examinations for	161
Professional and artistic schools proposed	51
Professors to wear gowns	9, 155
" to attend all examinations	9
" to have control of expenditures for their departments	10, 11, 12, 19, 101
" to attend daily prayers	14
" of school of law and medicine to be named in catalogue	18
" to attend public exhibitions	24
" to have right of burial in college lot at Greenwood	42
" to hold their titles, etc., liable to modifications	49
" invited to suggest improvements in college plan of education	49
" of science to report annual advancement of their subjects, proposed	52
" number of hours of attendance of	55, 117
" to lecture in university course	55
" in university course, to make examinations	60
" to receive fees in university course	61, 63
" to make catalogue of apparatus under their charge	66
" certain, to lecture in law school	67
" exempt from certain library regulations	79, 82
" allowed to prepare merit rolls of classes under them	87
" certain, to instruct in mining school	99, 100
" duties of certain, about to be appointed	118
" assignment of subjects to	119
" extra-collegiate occupations of, to be inquired into	121, 122
" emeritus, order of, created	123
" " privileges and honors of	123, 124
" " certain, elected	124, 125
" to have a reading room	125
" to pay for repairs of their houses	126
" to have discretionary power respecting reviews of studies	126
" sons of, exempt from paying tuition money	38
" salaries of—*see* " Appropriations for salaries."	
" for other particulars—*see* the various departments.	
Professorship of American history proposed	52
" of chemistry added to faculty of arts	118
" of geology proposed	52
" of law established	117
" " trustees to make regulations concerning	117
" of modern languages proposed	53
" of natural history and physiology proposed	52
" of physical and commercial geography proposed	52
Professorships, additional, proposed	50
" and professors	117
" order of emeritus, created	123
Property and revenues of the college, to be reported on by standing committee	139
" movable, inventory of, to be made	66

INDEX.

	PAGE
Railway engineering, instruction in, to be given	99
Reading room to be fitted up for professors	125
Real estate, expenditures for	35
Regents, report to, not to be entered on minutes	151
Registrar of the school of mines to be appointed	107
Regulations concerning examinations and prizes in law school	68—72
" for support of law school	72, 73
" for the library	75, 78
" for school of mines to be prepared	91
" concerning seminary prizes	114, 115
" and statutes, observance of, to be reported on by standing committee	139
Religion, evidences of, by whom to be taught	113, 119
Removal of the college	48, 162
Rent for school of law	34, 72
" house, allowance to professors for	118, 128, 129, 130
Rents, arrears of, standing committee to look after	140, 143
" " treasurer to collect	144
Repairs, appropriation for	33, 34
" of law school to be paid by the college	72
" committee on, to be annually appointed	126
" of houses of president and professors to be paid by themselves	126
" necessary, standing committee authorized to direct	140
" of houses of Drs. Torrey and Joy to be made	162
Report, annual, of the librarian	81, 83
" on annual advancement of science, proposed	52
Reports of professors on apparatus to be filed	66
" of committees of trustees to be in writing	149
" " " to be entered on minutes	149
" " " to be accompanied by resolutions	149
" of various committees—*see* the committees.	
Resident students, expediency of providing for	48
Resolutions of board of trustees, president to make synopsis of	7
" and rules of the board, clerk to collect	149
Retrenchment measures of 1861	31, 128
Revelation and science, mutual connection and support of, proposed to be taught	51
Revenues of the college to be reported upon by standing committee	139
Reviews of studies, how to be conducted	126
Rhetoric, tutor in, to be under direction of president	118
Rolls of merit	18, 87
Room to be fitted up for a keeper of meteorological observations	87
" " as a place of resort for college instructors	125
" to be provided for libraries of college societies	138
Rooms for resident students, expediency of providing	48
" to be set apart in college for mining school	90
" for lyceum of natural history granted	111

INDEX.

	PAGE
Rules of order of board of trustees	146—149
" and resolutions of board of trustees, clerk to collect	149

Safe to be provided for clerk of trustees.. 109
Salaries, titles, etc., of professors to be held liable to modifications....... 49
    " of certain professors to be appointed fixed...................... 118
    " " " " " when to take effect........ 119
    " inquiry as to the amount that ought to be paid................. 127
    " " whether they should depend on fees............... 127
    " made payable quarterly 127
    " amounts deducted from, to be refunded....................... 129
    " of college officers—*see* "Appropriations for salaries."
Salary of professor Lieber to be paid out of the general fund............ 130
Schemes of study and attendance—*see* "Attendance."
Scholarships, free—*see* "Free scholarships."
Scholarships in university course..52, 56
    " Moffat... 135
    " prize—*see* "Prize scholarships."
Scholarships and fellowships, appropriation for.......................... 33
School, grammar—*see* "Grammar school."
School of jurisprudence—*see* "Jurisprudence."
    " law—*see* "Law."
    " letters—*see* "Letters."
    " mines—*see* "Mines."
    " science—*see* "Science."
    " practical science, propriety of establishing..................... 63
Schools, free scholarships allowed certain................................. 134
    " separate professorial and artistic proposed.................... 50
Science, bachelor of, proposed to bestow degree of..................... 53
    " elective course of, for senior class..........................53, 55, 63
    " to be duly recognized in revised course of instruction........... 50
    " physical and natural, annual advancement of, proposed to be reported. 52
    " propriety of establishing school of practical..................... 63
    " school of, in university course, adopted......................... 55
    " " lectures in, by whom given..........................55, 60
    " " subjects to be taught in............................... 58
    " " instruction in, where given........................... 60
Science and art of education to be taught.............................. 59
Science and revelation, mutual connection and support of, proposed to be taught 51
Scientific collections, etc., room for, in new college buildings.............. 51
Seal of the college, adopted by governors of King's college............... 133
    " " new, adopted by regents of the university..........133, 165
    " " original, adopted by trustees of Columbia 133, 165
    " " exergue of.. 133
    " " to be engraved and transferred....................... 134
    " " detailed account of 162
    " " description of the device of 163

INDEX.

	PAGE
Seal of the college to be affixed to certain documents :	
" to leases executed by standing committee	16, 23, 139
" to diplomas for honorary degrees	25
" to diplomas for degrees in the law school	71
" to certificates of law school prizes	71
" to a memorial respecting land grants by congress	93
" to communications to certain schools and to certain authorities	94
" to agreements with tenants respecting party walls	142
" to certain modifications of leases	142, 143
" to certain instruments relating to investments	143
" to warrants required by treasurer for collection of rent	144
" to appointments of attorneys by treasurer	145
Secretary, president authorized to appoint	112
Secretary of the president to be paid monthly	133
Secret societies, inquiry as to their suppression	138
Semi-annual exhibition, college societies to be represented in	24
" " to be discontinued	24, 31, 116
Seminary prizes founded by Dr. McVickar	114, 115
Senior class allowed to visit manufacturing works, etc.	22
" allowed three courses of elective study	55
" three courses of elective study for, discontinued	63
" number of hours of attendance of	54
" to be instructed in constitutional law	118
Sessions, length of, in university course	60
" " in mining school	103
Sinking fund provided for	33
" to be invested	35
Site for astronomical observatory, committee on, appointed	111
" " " obtainable in central park	112
" for a church to be reserved in botanical garden property	14, 22
" for college buildings to be designated in botanical garden property	17
" " " to be elsewhere sought	17, 162
Smithsonian institution, donation of minerals of	92
" " thanks to	92
" " agreement with, respecting minerals	136
" minerals, appropriation for classifying	137
Societies, college, appropriation for	33, 137
" " to be represented at semi-annual exhibition	24
" " to have room for their libraries	138
" secret, inquiry as to their suppression	138
Society for promotion of religion and learning, prize scholarship of	113
" " " " to have two free scholarships	114
Sophomore class, to be taught elementary chemistry	118
" " to attend in german	110
Spanish, professorship of, proposed	53
" classes in, to be formed when expedient	57, 110
Special committees of trustees to be appointed by chairman	149
" examination for honors proposed	157
" meetings of trustees, inquiry as to authority and practice of	150

	PAGE
Specimens, mineralogical and geological, appropriation for	101
Sports and games of students, provision for	138

Standing committee :
 " appointment of... 138
 " duties of... 139
 " to report condition of botanic garden property 14
 " to contract loan for regulating botanic garden property........... 14
 " report concerning leasing botanic garden property................ 15
 " to prepare blank leases for botanic garden property.............. 16
 " to execute leases for botanic garden property................... 16
 " to report concerning temporary accommodations for college....... 16
 " to designate site for college in botanic garden property.......... 17
 " reserve lots for a church in botanic garden property............. 22
 " authorized to lease the reserved lots............................ 23
 " report concerning transfer of students from class to class........ 30
 " recommend discontinuance of separate account of Gebhard fund... 37
 " to select lot in Greenwood cemetery 41, 42
 " report concerning burials in the college lot..................... 42
 " to put in order Dr. Torrey's house.........................43, 162
 " to report concerning gymnastic exercises........................ 89
 " to audit accounts for broken apparatus......................... 102
 " to relieve dean of mining school from certain expenses.......... 103
 " to provide reading-room for college instructors................. 125
 " authorized to set apart playground in the upper estate........... 138
 " to be appointed by ballot....................................... 139
 " time of service of members..................................... 139
 " authorized to consent to transfer of leases..................139, 141
 " minutes of, to be read at stated meetings of trustees 139
 " to audit and authorize payment of bills for ordinary supplies...... 140
 " to direct necessary repairs..................................... 140
 " authorized to sell a certain lot of stone 140
 "   " to apply to legislature for certain powers.............. 140
 "   " to petition city corporation to fence certain lots........ 140
 "   " to prosecute for arrears of rent. etc..............140, 141
 "   " to compound with certain tenants.................141, 143
 " consent of, to transfer of leases, confirmed..................... 141
 " authorized, with treasurer, to agree to extension of time on college bonds.. 141
 " to audit bills for departments of instruction, before paid.......... 141
 " authorized to dismiss certain agents and employ others........... 141
 "   " to agree for erection of party walls.................... 142
 "   " to modify certain leases on conditions 142
 "   " to place a tablet in anteroom of library 142
 "   " to empower treasurer to invest certain moneys........ 142
 "   " to empower treasurer to convert certain investments... 142
 "   " to waive forfeiture of certain leases................... 143
 "   " to lease lots between 49th and 50th streets............ 143
 "   " to repair president's house........................... 143

INDEX.

	PAGE
Standing committee :	
" authorized to enforce rights of college as to arrears of rents........	143
" minutes of, not read, at special meetings of trustees..............	149
" authorized to repair houses of professors Torrey and Joy..........	162
Stated meetings of trustees, inquiry as to practice and authority of	150
Statute regulating the course of study, adopted...........................	55
Statutes, observance of, to be reported upon by standing committee........	139
Statutes of trustees, interleaved, to be kept on table at trustees' meetings....	145
Stocks, bonds, etc., treasurer to collect interest on	145
Strong, George T., donation of, to mining school.........................	92
" " thanks to	92
Students admitted after opening of college, fees of......................	30
" transfer of, to higher class, fees of.............................	30
" " " conditions requisite for...............	144
Studies, reviews of, how conducted.......................................	126
Study, statute on course of, adopted	55
" elective course of, for senior class.............................55,	63
" additional subjects of, in law school............................67,	73
" five courses of, in mining school, authorized.......................	108
" and attendance, schemes of—*see* "Attendance."	
Subjects in university course assigned to college officers...................	56
" to be taught in the schools of the university course...............	58
" of study, additional, in the law school..........................67,	73
" assigned to the several professors, 1857...........................	119
Supplies, appropriation for...............................12, 13, 33, 34,	101
" bills for ordinary, standing committee to direct payment of........	140
Support of law school, regulations for...................................72,	73
" of mining school, appropriation for.......................96, 97,	100
Surplus income to be set apart as a sinking fund.........................	33
" " to be invested...	35
Surrender of leases allowed in certain cases...................... 141,	143
Surveying instruments, appropriation for..................................	11
" appropriation for department of...............................12,	33
Sym, John, tablet to, to be placed in anteroom of library..................	142
Tax, for water in president's house	165
Taxes, appropriation for..	35
" etc., arrears of, standing committee to look after..................	141
Tenants, certain, allowed to compound for rent, etc....................141,	143
" " " to surrender lease....................141,	143
" " agreement with, respecting party walls..................	142
" " allowed modification of leases......................142,	143
" " " extension of time for building,...................	142
Tenure of office for instructors in university course......................59,	60
Terms of instruction in mining school.....................................	103
" " university course........	60
Text-book in ancient geography, president to report......................	65
" books to be used in department of physics..........................	64
Time of meeting of board of trustees..................................145,	150

	PAGE
Time of anniversary meeting of governors fixed by charter	162
Title of chair of chemistry in mining school changed	100
" of Dr. Lieber's professorship in law school fixed	74
Titles of professors of college instructing in mining school	100
" salaries, etc., of professors to be held liable to modifications	49
Torrey, Dr. John, herbarium and library of, accepted	43
" " house to be put in order for	43, 162
" " granted extension of time to reside in house	44
Transfer of leases, standing committee authorized to consent to	139, 144
" of students from class to class, conditions of	30, 144
Treasurer, appropriation for office of	33
" to confer with standing committee about management of funds	139
" accounts to be audited by standing committee	139
" authorized to agree to extension of time on college bonds	141
" authorized to substitute new bonds for old ones	141
" not to pay certain bills till audited by standing committee	141
" authorized to invest certain moneys	142
" authorized to convert certain investments	142
" authorized to collect rent in arrears	144
" authorized to receive tuition fees	144
" authorized to employ attorneys	145
" authorized to receive interest on stocks, etc	145
" to pay an account for making and altering a seal	165
" to pay annual water tax on president's house	166
" to have table-drawers in trustees' room subdivided	166
Trustees, president to make synopsis of resolutions of board of	7
" minutes of board of, from 1784 to 1787, demanded	109
" demand for minutes of, not complied with	109
" copy of minutes of, to be sent to regents of university	109
" minutes of, to be transcribed	109
" meetings of, not to be disturbed by entrance of persons	120, 166
" forfeiture of seat of any, from absence	145
" new statutes of, to be kept on table at meetings	145
" day, hour, and place of meeting of the board of	145, 146
" rules of order at meetings of	146—149
" order of business at meetings of	146
" clerk to collect permanent rules and resolutions in force	149
" stated and special meetings of, authority for holding	150
" report of, to regents, not to be entered on minutes	151
" table-drawers of, to be provided with keys	166
" table-drawers of, to be for their exclusive use	166
Tuition fees—see "Fees.'	
Tuition, free—see "Free tuition."	
Tutor in rhetoric and belles-lettres, to be under direction of the president	118
" english literature appointed	152
" greek and latin appointed	152
" mathematics appointed	152
Tutors, expediency of appointing one or more inquired into	151

INDEX.

	PAGE
Tutors, faculty recommend appointment of four	151, 152
" to have a seat at college board on certain occasions	152
" to have no vote	152
" three ordered to be appointed	152

Undergraduate course of instruction—*see* "Instruction."
University convocation, faculty authorized to send delegates to 153
    " regents of, right of visitation not recognized 86
University course—*see* "Instruction."

Vacations, propriety of allowing president discretion respecting 44
    " in school of mines 104
Visitation of the college, committee of trustees for 28, 153
    " " " right of regents to, not admitted 86

Walls, party, agreement as to erection of 142
Weights, etc., memorial in favor of uniform system of 154
Working laboratory proposed to be erected 20, 46
    " " permitted at the college 20, 46
    " " regulations concerning 20, 21

Year, fiscal, when to terminate 144

Printed in Dunstable, United Kingdom